see SPOT RUN

QUARRY

Kirsten Cole-MacMurray and Stephanie Nishimoto

see
SPOT
RUN

100 Ways to Work Out with Your Dog

BEVERLY MASSACHUSETTS

QUARRY BOOKS

First published in the United States of America by
Quarry Books, a member of
Quayside Publishing Group
100 Cummings Center
Suite 406-L
Beverly, Massachusetts 01915-6101
Telephone: (978) 282-9590
Fax: (978) 283-2742
www.quarrybooks.com

Library of Congress Cataloging-in-Publication Data available

ISBN-13: 978-1-59253-614-6
ISBN-10: 1-59253-614-X

10 9 8 7 6 5 4 3 2 1

Design: Laura H. Couallier, Laura Herrmann Design
Cover Images: iStockphoto.com, front, spine (bottom); Lind Fund, spine (top);
             Pam Marks, back
Photography by Pam Marks unless otherwise indicated.
Illustration on page 13, Gayle Isabelle Ford

Printed in China

Dedication

For Chelsea and Caelin—

Kirsten's first agility dogs that started her down the path to train dogs and instruct other dog lovers. Chelsea gave her the first Toprock litter, and achieved the title of ASCA Hall of Fame Dam with that first litter. Caelin was a four-time winner of the ASCA National Specialty Most Versatile Aussie competition, achieving the highest combined score in agility, obedience, conformation, and stock work.

Toprock Team (Caelin's puppies) on the way home from the ASCA National Specialty, October, 2009.

Contents

Foreword
by Dr. Ian Gordon Holsworth

Man and dog, dog and man: linked forever by man's need for companionship and dog's ability to fulfill that role. We have lived with them since prehistoric times, shared the cave, hut, humpy, teepee, and tent. The dog's position within our family and society has continued to evolve along with us. The dog's present role is as companion, family member, and playmate.

Modern society has changed significantly in the last century. We live in bigger cities, have less personal space, rely on electronic media for our entertainment, are less physically active, and spend less time outdoors. These changes have affected our health and the health of our canine friends. We are less fit, more overweight, and more sedentary. Our dogs are too.

In *See Spot Run*, Kirsten Cole-MacMurray and Stephanie Nishimoto have skillfully demonstrated how we can begin to correct some of the imbalances we all face in our lives: the battle between work and play, relaxation and activity, sloth and fitness. By turning to our trusted canine companions and spending active time with them we can teach them skills and walk, run, and play with them. In turn, this process will enrich our lives, improve our own fitness, and take them on our journey toward better health, happiness, and balance.

Offered in Part I are comprehensive indoor fitness activities that emphasize core musculature and balance skills. In Part II, outdoor activities that develop speed, strength, and endurance are featured. The range and variety of dog athletic activities are well introduced, and we are given many suggestions on how to participate. Part III offers a brief overview of nutrition, illness, and injury prevention, plus broad recommendations for when your pet begins his or her more active, athletic lifestyle.

Adding this book to our "dog library" will allow us to educate ourselves and actively pursue a more complete bond with our pets. This strategy is bound to improve both our own and our dog's fitness and health. Following just a few of the suggestions in *See Spot Run* will allow both you and your

Born in Canada and raised in Australia, Dr. Ian Gordon Holsworth was educated at several prestigious universities in Australia and is an examined member of the surgery college of the Australian College of Veterinary Scientists. Dr. Holsworth has been at Veterinary Medical and Surgical Group in Ventura, California, since 2003. With his professional ties to U.C. Davis Veterinary Orthopedic surgery department, he is active in clinical research and works on challenging surgical cases with the university. He is a leading instructor in canine knee reconstruction and arthroscopic surgery and remains very active in veterinary continuing education around the world.

dog to discover and participate in fun and varied athletic activities. There is no time like now to change the way you and your canine companion live your life.

— Dr. Ian Gordon Holsworth, BSc BVSc (Hons) MACVSc (Surgery) Diplomate ACVS

Introduction to Canine Physical Fitness

Keeping dogs physically fit is important for their health and well-being. Overall health and fitness are not only essential for dogs to be able to excel at sports, but also to ensure a dog will live long with a good quality of life. Dogs age at a rate seven times faster than humans do and can succumb to many of the same life-threatening conditions that plague people. In return for their dogs' unconditional love and loyalty, dog owners need to provide their four-legged companions with a lifestyle that promotes longevity and freedom from debilitating illness and pain.

First and foremost, dogs need to use their muscles and mind to stay fit, alert, and healthy.

This entails more than having a backyard or another dog friend for stimulation and fitness; the owner must be physically involved, too. This book will explore sports and other activities to provide an active lifestyle, as well as fun exercises to help prevent canine injuries while playing.

The goal of any conditioning program for dogs should be to strengthen muscles, build endurance, and maintain flexibility. The body has two types of muscle fibers: *fast-twitch* and *slow-twitch*. Fast-twitch muscle fibers are used for short-term strength—to provide acceleration and power. Slow-twitch muscle fibers are used for long-term endurance, such as in distance running or swimming. Strengthening exercises build up the fast-twitch fibers in the muscles; endurance exercises build up the slow-twitch muscle fibers; and stretching exercises maintain the flexibility of both kinds of muscle fibers. This book offers all three kinds of exercises, and more.

How to Get Motivated

Exercise should be fun for both dog and owner. To encourage your dog to learn something new, guide him through the step-by-step process with enthusiasm, patience, and lots of motivational rewards. Dogs enjoy doing things they know how to do well and that have a palpable payoff. You will also reap benefits from increasing your dog's fitness: once you make a commitment to exercising with your dog, more and more often you will find yourself getting up off the couch, into the great outdoors, and breathing fresh air. Exercise thus provides both you and your dog with physical and mental stimulation.

Training together also helps the human-dog bond grow stronger and more intimate. Dogs are pack animals; they look for leadership from their owner. Training and bonding with your dog helps define your role as the pack leader for your pet while developing your confidence in assuming that essential leadership role.

Before You Begin

1. Check with your veterinarian to make sure your dog is fit enough to start a conditioning program. The dog's age, weight, and health history will determine how to proceed.
2. Start slowly. Don't expect the dog to be able to do the exercises right away. Reward often to shape the correct behavior.
3. Keep your sessions short and fun. Don't work the dog to the point of fatigue.

All conditioning programs should begin with a low activity level and increase as the dog's fitness progresses. Overworking muscles can cause painful injuries, including sprains and tears to the muscles, tendons, and ligaments. Always evaluate a dog's overall fitness before starting an intense workout program.

Canine Muscle Groups

Exercises to strengthen and stretch muscles should focus on three sections of the dog's body: the **front**, the **core**, and the **rear**. Dogs rely on these three main muscle groups for most of their physical activity. It is important to strengthen all three sections, so make sure you do not fall into the habit of choosing exercises that only focus on one group.

Keeping their muscles healthy, strong, and flexible from nose to tail will greatly aid dogs in preventing injuries and provide support for maintaining a good quality of life into their senior years.

The **front** muscle group includes the neck, shoulders, upper arms, and lower arms. The **core** muscles are found in the back and the abdomen. The **rear** muscle group includes the pelvis, upper legs, and lower legs.

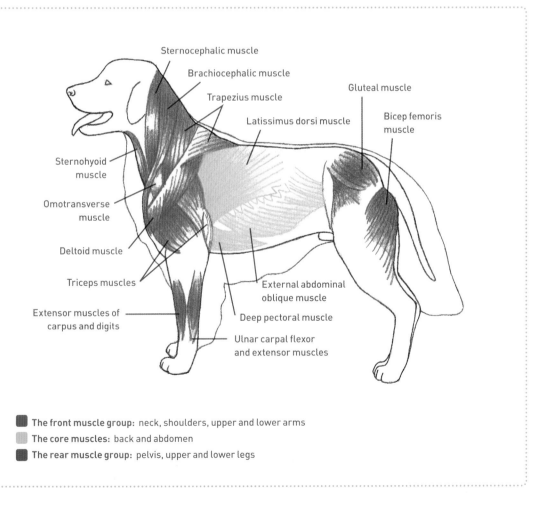

Sternocephalic muscle
Brachiocephalic muscle
Trapezius muscle
Gluteal muscle
Latissimus dorsi muscle
Bicep femoris muscle
Sternohyoid muscle
Omotransverse muscle
Deltoid muscle
Triceps muscles
External abdominal oblique muscle
Extensor muscles of carpus and digits
Deep pectoral muscle
Ulnar carpal flexor and extensor muscles

The front muscle group: neck, shoulders, upper and lower arms
The core muscles: back and abdomen
The rear muscle group: pelvis, upper and lower legs

PART I

FUN
FITNESS
exercise

Strengthening Exercises

The first step in planning a fitness program is to take stock of where you are. The physical condition of the dog and owner should be objectively assessed by a veterinarian and doctor. Any condition that would affect physical activity must be discussed with a professional.

Next, set some goals. Is it to become fit or to retain fitness? Is it to get stronger or to run faster and longer? Or is it to avoid strained muscles? Is there a sport or an activity you'd like to participate in that requires building up specific muscle groups? Write them down and post them somewhere to remind you why you need to get out and get going.

Begin with strengthening exercises to help build fast-twitch muscle fibers, which will improve a dog's quickness and agility.

Start working on these exercises slowly, with only one or two repetitions, increasing by one or two repetitions after a week. Muscles also need time to recover, so do not do these exercises daily, especially when first starting. Take a day off between sessions.

As the dog becomes more physically fit and the exercises become easier to execute, they can be made more challenging by increasing the duration of the *hold position*, or increasing the number of repetitions of the exercise. Doing the exercise in conjunction with hill work or adding a Pilates ball will make things more exciting for the fit dog!

Which exercises in Part I would you and your dog enjoy? Try them with your pet. Remember to use positive reinforcement techniques and to reward frequently for each successful small step in training the correct behavior. Keep sessions short and fun. It is not necessary to be able to do all the exercises or to include all the exercises in your program. Pick the ones that fit your goals and that are enjoyable for both you and your dog to do.

1. Sit Up or Beg

To sit up, or beg, the dog must sit up and raise both front feet at the same time. This exercise strengthens the back, hindquarters, and abdominal muscles—the core and rear muscles of the dog's body. Holding the sit position builds strength in the rear legs. Balancing on the rear builds abdominal strength.

Learning the behavior may be easier for smaller dogs; however, teaching it to large dogs can pay greater health dividends in their senior years. From the sit position, bring a treat up above the dog's head, close to his nose, until the dog lifts his front feet off the ground. Use a verbal cue ("Sit up") and reward the dog for progressive small increments in lifting his front feet off the ground, until he is holding the position in a sit-up. Take care to bring the treat straight upward from the nose. Moving it forward or backward may cause the dog to fall in either direction. Larger dogs can be helped by placing them with their back against a corner of the room, so they can use the walls to balance themselves.

Go slowly when training with this exercise. Don't expect the dog to sit up and hold the position right away. Reward progressive small increments of his raising himself up until he is sitting squarely on his haunches. Then lengthen the time before giving the treat, until he can hold the position for 10 seconds.

step 1

step 2

step 3

1. Start with the dog in a sit position.
2. Bring a tasty treat straight up from his nose.
3. Raise the treat until his front feet are off the ground.

2. Wave or High Five

Strengthening the muscles of the shoulder and upper arm can help canine athletes avoid shoulder injuries. These muscles are required to absorb the impact of the dog's full weight at the completion of a jump or contact obstacle.

This exercise helps strengthen the shoulder and upper arm. The greatest benefit is gained from teaching the dog to reach up with her whole arm, keeping the pastern (wrist area) straight. Progress gradually during training sessions, to rewarding for your hand held up in the air as far as the dog can reach. Be sure to work each arm of the dog, to develop both sides evenly.

step 1

step 2

1. Enclose a tasty treat in one hand and hold it directly in front of a sitting dog.
2. Wait for the dog to paw at the hand for the treat.
3. Begin by rewarding the dog for pawing at the hand when it is held low.
4. Gradually raise your hand until the dog is reaching to paw at your hand while the treat is held high.

step 3

step 4

3. Beg and Wave

This exercise strengthens all three main sections of the dog: front (shoulder and foreleg), core (back and abdomen), and rear (hindquarters). Once the dog is able to do the individual beg and wave exercises separately, put them together to work all three sections of his body at one time. As the dog reaches for the treat hand, raise it higher and farther out to extend his arm.

step 1

1. Begin with the dog sitting in front of you.
2. Bring the dog up into a beg position, and hold the treat higher so the dog reaches with his forearm.

step 2

4. Stand-Down-Stand

step 1

This exercise also strengthens all three main sections of the dog's body at once. It is easy to teach and simple for all types and sizes of dogs to learn to do. Begin by enclosing a tasty treat in a hand held in front of the dog when she is in a stand position. Move the treat down toward the dog, between her front legs. She will collapse backward into a down position, like an accordion. Once the dog is lying down, raise the treat so she will pop back up into a standing position, without moving any of her paws. Start with three repetitions and slowly build up to between five and ten repetitions, depending on the age of the dog and the fitness level desired. Remember to keep it fun and rewarding for the dog.

step 2

1. Begin with the dog in a stand position. Enclose a tasty treat in a hand held in front of her nose.
2. Lower the treat between the dog's legs.
3. The dog should rock backward into a down position.
4. Guide the dog back into a stand position by raising the treat upward and a little forward. Place the other hand under the dog to support her in a standing position.
5. Reward and praise the dog when she is able to stand unsupported by your hand.

step 3   step 4   step 5

5. Crawl

This exercise strengthens the forelimbs, abdominals, and rear limb muscles. Teaching a dog to crawl is easy because it is a natural, instinctive movement. Begin with the dog lying down with all four elbows on the ground. For smaller dogs, sit on the floor in front of the dog with your knees up and your feet flat on the ground. Use a tasty treat to lure the dog through the gap between the floor and your legs. He will follow the treat in a crawl position. For larger dogs, set up a series of poles or line up several four-legged chairs, and lure the dog to crawl through the gap underneath them.

step 1

1. Sit on the floor with the dog lying facing the gap between the floor and your upraised knees. Give a verbal cue ("Crawl") and use a tasty treat to lure him into crawling into the gap between the floor and your knees. Keep the treat low to the ground.

2. Continue to enclose the treat in your hand while guiding the dog through the gap, keeping the treat low to the ground to encourage crawling.

3. Give a release word ("Okay!") as the dog goes completely through the gap, then reward him with the treat.

step 2

step 3

6. Roll Over

Most dogs love rolling over and many wiggle on their back naturally, which is a precursor to the full roll over. It's fun for the dog, entertaining for spectators, and a good strengthening exercise for the core muscles (back and abdominals) and neck.

step 1

Begin the session with the dog lying down with all four of her elbows on the ground. Hold a tasty treat at the end of her nose and lure her head toward her hip. The object is to get her to rock over onto the opposite hip, while reaching for the treat held at the first hip. As the dog reaches, she will lie on her side, following the treat. Move the treat across the dog's back, behind her hip, and she will roll over, reaching for the treat. Reward the dog for each step of the behavior until she can complete the whole behavior. Remember to roll both sides—to the right and to the left—an equal number of repetitions.

step 2

1. Enclose a tasty treat in a hand held near the dog's nose.
2. Use a verbal cue ("Roll over") and move the treat along one side of the dog, toward her hip. She will shift her weight to the hip on the opposite side, as her head follows the treat.
3. Move the treat across the dog's back, behind her hip. She will roll over, still following the treat.
4. Reward and praise your dog when she has rolled over completely.

step 3

step 4

7. Turning

Turning is a fun exercise that is easy to teach with a treat. Turning strengthens the front limbs and neck and improves back flexibility. As the dog stands in front, facing you, place a treat in front of his nose to get him to follow the treat hand around in a circle as you pivot in place, turning the dog to the left if you use your left hand or to the right with your right hand. Be sure to train your dog to turn a complete circle in both directions. Reward each time the dog completes the circle.

step 1

1. Stand the dog in front of you, facing you.

2. Hold a tasty treat in front of his nose. Give a verbal cue ("Turn") and have the dog follow the treat hand in a circle around you as you pivot. Remember to turn the dog to the left with your left hand, or to the right with your right hand.

3. Reward as the dog completes the circle.

step 2

step 3

8. Treat Reach

The treat reach is a dog version of human crunches or sit-ups. This exercise focuses on the dog's abdominal muscles and strengthens the core muscle groups. Lay the dog down on her side in a relaxed position with her head on the ground. Enclosing a tasty treat in one hand, lure her nose toward the side of her rib cage, then back down to the floor in resting position. Keeping your hand where pictured will allow you to feel the abdominal muscles tighten and loosen. Start with two repetitions on each side and increase slowly.

step 1

1. Enclose a treat in one hand. Lay the dog down on her side in a relaxed position with her head on the ground. Position your other hand in front of her top rear leg.

2. With the treat hand, lure the dog's nose toward the side of her rib cage as close as is comfortable for her.

step 2

> When doing strengthening exercises, use training treats for stationary exercises, such as stand and down, and use toys for exercises of motion, such as uphill retrieve and tugging.

9. Walking Backward

This exercise is simple to teach and strengthens the core and rear muscle groups. Stand facing the dog. Enclose a tasty treat in one hand in front of his nose. Step toward the dog; he will back up instinctively as you move toward him. Initially reward one or two steps he takes backward, and then increase the number of steps as the dog becomes proficient at the backward movement. A great time to do this exercise is at feeding time. Simply move toward the dog with his bowl in your hand and reward with some of the food in the bowl when the dog moves backward. To increase the difficulty of the exercise, increase the distance the dog has to back up to receive the treat, or try having him back uphill.

step 1

1. Begin by facing the dog, a tasty treat enclosed in one hand.
2. Give a verbal cue ("Back up") and move toward the dog, causing him to back up. Reward him.
3. Increase the number of steps he needs to take backward before he receives his treat.

step 2

step 3

10. Tug

One of a dog's favorite, classic games is tug. Most dogs tug naturally. It is a fantastic front and rear muscle group strengthener, specifically working the neck, front legs, back, and rear leg muscles. Start the exercise with a verbal cue ("Tug"). Keep the tug toy low so the dog does not lift off the ground to tug. Train an end to the game with a release word ("Give").

If your dog does not like to tug, you can teach her to tug with a treat tug. Use an old sock and fill it with tasty treats. The dog will want to taste the treats through the material and will bite the treat sock. Slowly build the biting and nibbling of the sock into tugging. Make sure when you are tugging not to pull so aggressively that you rip the tug toy out of the dog's mouth. Only apply enough tugging force to keep your dog thinking she can win the tug-of-war.

Most dogs love to tug. Keep it a fun game by training verbal cues to start and stop the game.

11. Digging

Digging strengthens the front muscle groups. Many dogs like to dig naturally (and will do so when given the opportunity!). You probably do not want to encourage random digging, but making digging a special activity in a specific area will give your dog exercise and will focus his digging efforts at a time and place designated by you. A child's sandbox or a homemade box of sand in the yard can serve as a great place to focus the digging exercise. Control the behavior by giving a verbal cue ("Dig") to start and stop ("Enough") the exercise.

Digging is a great exercise to strengthen a dog's front muscle groups (shoulders, front legs, and neck).

1. Take the dog to the sandbox and bring along a toy or bag of tasty treats.
2. Lay the toy or treats on top of the sand and encourage the dog to retrieve the reward.
3. Each time the toy or treat is placed back on the sand, cover it with more sand until it is actually buried and the dog must dig it out.
4. Add a verbal command to the behavior ("Dig" or "Find it") and bury the treasure deeper each time, so he has to dig longer to get the reward.

Choose a slight slope with plenty of room for the dog to run up for the toy and circle back. Keep plenty of water available and stop the game *before* the dog is ready to stop; don't wait until she is exhausted.

12. Retrieve Uphill

Retrieving is a great form of exercise. Retrieving uphill is an excellent strengthening exercise that works the lower limb muscles. If your dog is not a natural retriever, you can use a toy to encourage the game. Using a leash on the dog will help teach her to return with the toy. Once you have your dog retrieving reliably, toss the toy up a slope or hill and have her retrieve it. Running uphill builds strength and endurance.

13. Diagonal Leg Lifts

step 1

Diagonal leg lifts strengthen the dog's neck, shoulders, and back, and help improve core strength and balance. With the dog standing in a perpendicular position, hold the nearest front foot and the farthest hind foot at the ankles. Slowly raise the front and rear feet off the ground several inches so that the dog is balancing on two legs. Hold the position for 5 to 10 seconds, gradually increasing the length of time as the dog strengthens. Be sure to repeat this exercise on both sets of legs to keep your dog's strength equal on both sides.

1. Position your dog to stand perpendicular to you.
2. Raise one of the dog's front legs off the ground.
3. Raise the dog's opposite hind leg off the ground.

step 2

step 3

Pilates Ball Strengthening Exercises

As with humans, using a Pilates ball with your dog is an excellent way to strengthen her core muscle group and increase her balance and body awareness. You can use a round Pilates ball, a peanut-shaped ball, or a stability disk (also known as a balance cushion). When using a Pilates ball or peanut, have a friend help you keep the ball from rolling, or place the ball between you and a wall to keep it stabilized.

Place the Pilates ball or peanut against a wall to stabilize it when working alone with a dog.

14. Circling the Ball with Front Legs Up

Use the Pilates ball for this exercise, or have the dog go around one end of the Pilates peanut. Holding a treat, encourage the dog to place his front feet on the ball as his back feet remain on the ground. Once he is comfortable in the position, sidestep against him to get him to move sideways around the ball while his front feet remain on the ball and the back feet on the floor. Be sure to have him circle the ball in both directions.

1. Use a tasty treat to encourage the dog to put his front feet on the Pilates ball.
2. Sidestep into the dog to move him sideways around the ball.
3. Use lots of praise as well as tasty treats to make this a fun exercise.

step 1

step 2

step 3

15. Balancing on the Ball

Small dogs can balance on a Pilates ball, but larger dogs require a Pilates peanut. Ask someone to help stabilize the ball for the dog, or use a wall to stabilize the ball. Use a treat to encourage your dog to climb onto the Pilates ball or peanut with all four feet on the ball at the same time. Reward him for balancing on the ball for 5 to 10 seconds, increasing the time as the dog becomes stronger. To increase the difficulty of this exercise, increase the duration of time or gently rock the ball, forcing the dog to work harder at balancing.

step 1

1. Use a treat to encourage the dog to place his front feet on the ball.
2. Have the dog get up onto the ball with all four feet, and reward him with the treat.
3. By pausing to issue the treat, encourage the dog to balance for a greater length of time on the ball.

step 2

step 3

16. Diagonal Leg Lifts on the Ball

Once the dog is comfortable balancing on the ball or peanut with all four feet, make the balancing act more difficult by adding diagonal leg lifts (see page 29; the dog should already have learned to do these on the ground). Begin with the dog standing on the Pilates ball. Slowly raise his nearest front foot and farthest hind foot off the ball by several inches, so that he is balancing on two legs. Hold for 5 to 10 seconds, gradually increasing the time as the dog gets stronger. Be sure to alternate both sets of legs to keep the dog's strength balanced.

step 1

1. Have your dog balance on the ball.
2. Raise the dog's front leg off the ball.
3. Raise the dog's opposite hind leg off the ball.

step 2

step 3

17. Stand-Down-Stand on the Ball

Once the dog is comfortable standing and balancing on the ball or peanut, use a treat to lure him from the stand to the down position, then back into the standing position, while he maintains his balance on the ball. Start with three repetitions and increase gradually to five.

step 1

1. Have the dog stand on the ball on all four feet.
2. Lure him down by lowering the treat between his legs.
3. Reward the dog when he achieves the down position.
4. Guide the dog back into the stand position by enclosing another treat in your hand and raising the hand.
5. Reward the dog when he is again standing balanced on the ball.

step 2

step 3

step 4

step 5

Balance Cushion Exercises

18. Front Legs on the Balance Cushion

Use a tasty treat to lure the dog into placing her front legs
on the balance cushion with her back feet on the floor, then
holding that position. Reward the dog for standing with her
front legs on the cushion for longer durations.

Reward the dog for placing her
front legs on the cushion and
holding that position.

19. Hind Legs on the Balance Cushion

Use a tasty treat to have the dog back up and place her
hind legs on the balance cushion while keeping her front
legs on the floor. Reward the dog for holding the position for
longer durations.

Reward the dog for placing her
hind legs on the cushion and
balancing there.

20. Circling with Front Legs on the Cushion

Use a tasty treat to get the dog to place her front feet on the balance cushion with her back feet on the floor. Sidestep against the dog and continue to hold out the treat, to lure her into moving around the cushion, keeping her front feet on the cushion and her back feet on the floor. The dog should completely circle the cushion. Be sure to circle in both directions to keep her strength balanced.

1. Hold out a tasty treat to get the dog to put her front feet on the cushion.
2. Sidestep against the dog to move her along around the cushion.
3. Use lots of praise and tasty treats to make this a fun exercise.

step 1

step 2

step 3

21. Circling with Back Feet on the Cushion

Use a tasty treat to have the dog back up and place his back feet on the balance cushion, leaving his front feet on the floor. Sidestep against the dog and continue to hold out the treat, to lure him into moving around the cushion, keeping his back feet on the cushion and his front feet on the floor. The dog should completely circle the cushion. Be sure to circle in both directions to keep his strength balanced.

step 1

1. Hold out a tasty treat to encourage the dog to put his back feet on the cushion.
2. Sidestep into the dog to move him along around the cushion.
3. Use lots of praise and tasty treats to make this a fun exercise.

step 2

step 3

22. Sit to Stand with Front Feet on the Cushion

When the dog is comfortable with her front feet on the balance cushion, use a treat to have her sit, then stand, while keeping her front feet on the cushion.

step 1

1. Begin by having the dog put her front feet on the balance cushion.

2. Hold a tasty treat above her nose to get her to sit with her front feet on the cushion.

3. Continuing to offer the treat, have the dog stand up, keeping her front feet on the cushion, then reward her.

step 2

step 3

23. Sit to Stand with Back Feet on the Cushion

When the dog is comfortable with her back feet on the balance cushion, have her sit, then go to a stand, while keeping her back feet on the cushion.

step 1

1. Start with the dog's back feet on the cushion.
2. Hold out a tasty treat to encourage her to sit with her front feet on the floor and her back feet on the balance cushion.
3. Continue to offer the treat to have the dog stand up, keeping her back feet on the cushion, then reward her.

step 2

step 3

24. Stand to Down with Front Feet on the Cushion

When the dog is comfortable with her front feet on the cushion, have her lie down, then stand up, while keeping her front feet on the cushion.

step 1

1. Begin with the dog's front feet on the balance cushion.

2. Lower a tasty treat between the dog's front legs to encourage her to lie down with her front feet on the cushion.

3. Use the treat to lure the dog to stand up, keeping her front feet on the cushion, then reward her.

step 2

step 3

25. Stand to Down with Back Feet on the Cushion

When the dog is comfortable with her back feet on the cushion, ask her to lie down and then stand up while keeping her back feet on the cushion.

step 1

1. Begin by having the dog put her back feet on the balance cushion.
2. Lower a tasty treat between the dog's front legs to encourage her to lie down with her back feet on the cushion.
3. Use the treat to lure the dog to stand up, keeping her back feet on the cushion, then reward her.

step 2

step 3

26. Balancing with Four Feet on the Cushion

When the dog is comfortable placing her front feet and back feet on the balance cushion as separate exercises, ask her to step with all four feet onto the balance cushion and balance there. Hold for 5 to 10 seconds, increasing the time as the dog gets stronger by withholding the treat for longer periods.

step 1

1. Begin with the dog's front feet on the balance cushion.

2. Use a tasty treat to encourage the dog to get up onto the balance cushion with all four feet.

3. Encourage the dog to remain in a stand, balancing on the cushion.

step 2

step 3

27. Sit to Stand with Four Feet on the Cushion

When the dog is comfortable balancing with all four feet on the cushion, ask her to sit and then lure her back into a stand. Start with three to five repetitions, gradually increasing the time the dog is required to hold each position, as she gets stronger.

step 1

1. Have the dog stand on the balance cushion on all four feet.

2. Use a tasty treat to lure the dog into a sit position while balancing all four feet on the cushion.

3. Lure her back into a stand, using the treat.

step 2

step 3

28. Stand-Down-Stand with Four Feet on the Cushion

When the dog is comfortable balancing with all four feet on the cushion, ask her to lie down, and then lure her into a stand. Start with three to five repetitions, gradually increasing the time the dog is required to hold each position, as she gets stronger.

step 1

1. Have the dog stand on the balance cushion on all four feet.

2. Lower a tasty treat between the dog's front legs to encourage her to lie down while balancing with all four feet on the cushion.

3. Lure the dog back into a stand while still balancing all four feet on the cushion.

step 2

step 3

Building Endurance

Endurance exercises strengthen the cardiovascular system, sending more oxygen to the muscles, strengthening the slow-twitch muscles, and allowing the dog to exercise for longer intervals without experiencing fatigue.

Healthy adult dogs should participate in some form of endurance exercise at least three times a week. Do any of the following endurance exercises, varying the type and/or location of the activity to keep it interesting. Puppies under 18 months old should not do endurance exercises because their growth plates may not have closed. The pounding, repetitive motion required by these exercises can lead to bone and joint damage. Endurance exercises for senior dogs should be limited by the dog's general health and fitness. As with the previous exercises, begin with short sessions. Avoid injury by gradually working up to the recommended length of time. Be sure to check with your dog's veterinarian before starting any endurance program.

29. Biking

Most dogs enjoy running alongside a bicycle. It is best to bike on grass or a dirt trail or find a road with a shoulder area for bikes that allows the dog to trot alongside on grass or dirt. Biking with a dog on cement, asphalt, or other hard surfaces can cause joint damage. Use a harness when biking the dog to avoid injury to her back or neck. Although many people hold the leash in their hand with the handlebars when they bike, there are devices, such as a "springer," that mount to the bicycle and attach to the dog, enabling you to use both hands to steer and balance.

Training

Start at a walking or slow trotting pace for the dog to warm up. If she has not been allowed to potty before starting, during the first few minutes look for signs that she needs to go. (Be sure to pick up and dispose of dog defecation.) Increase the pace to a good trot for as long as the dog is comfortable. Gradually work up to biking with the dog at a trot for 15 to 20 continuous minutes. Trotting requires the dog to distribute her weight evenly on all four legs and therefore builds muscle evenly in all four legs. Allow the dog to cool down with a 5-minute slow trot or walk at the end of the outing.

Be aware of weather conditions, traffic, and most important, the physical state of the dog when biking with a dog.

30. Roller Skating or In-line Skating

This is a great activity for the owner and the dog to get fit together. Most dogs love running alongside their owner. Try to skate where the dog can run alongside on grass or dirt. Running on cement, asphalt, or other hard surfaces can cause joint damage to the dog. Be sure to use a harness on the dog to avoid neck and back injury.

Training

Start at a walking or slow trotting pace for the dog to warm up. If the dog has not been allowed to potty before starting, during the first few minutes look for signs that he needs to go. (Be sure to pick up and dispose of dog defecation.) Increase the pace to a good trot for as long as the dog is comfortable. Gradually work up to skating with the dog at a trot for 15 to 20 continuous minutes. Trotting requires the dog to distribute his weight evenly on all four legs and therefore builds muscle evenly in all four legs. Allow the dog to cool down with a 5-minute slow trot or walk at the end of the outing.

Just as when you are biking with your dog (see page 45), when skating you must be aware of weather conditions, traffic, and most important, the physical state of the dog.

31. Jogging

It is best to jog with a dog on grass, sand, or a dirt trail. Jogging on cement, asphalt, or other hard surfaces can cause joint damage to the dog—and it's not so great for the owner, either. The owner's fitness level must also be considered when jogging with the dog. If jogging is new to the owner, as with the dog, build up the distance and duration slowly.

Training

Start at a walking or slow trotting pace for the dog to warm up. If the dog has not been allowed to potty before starting, during the first few minutes look for signs that he needs to go. (Be sure to pick up and dispose of dog defecation.) Work up to a good trot and keep the pace constant for as long as the dog is comfortable. Gradually work up to jogging with the dog at a trot for 20 continuous minutes. Trotting requires the dog to distribute his weight evenly on all four legs and therefore builds muscle evenly in all four legs. Allow the dog to cool down with a 5-minute slow trot or walk at the end of the outing.

Find a beach that allows dogs and have a fun run with your dog. Remember to take along a plastic bag so you can pick up after your dog.

Interval jogging is a good place to start. Begin by walking for 1 minute and then jogging for 1 minute, alternating walking and jogging in 1-minute increments until a total of 20 minutes of exercise is reached. Gradually increase the time spent jogging until it lasts for 20 minutes.

32. Using a Treadmill

Consider teaching your dog to run on a treadmill for exercise during foul weather conditions, or when there is not enough time for a long walk or run. You must have a treadmill at home, or access to a friend's home gym, because most gyms will not allow your dog in the facility. Make sure the treadmill is at least twice the body length of the dog. Face the treadmill out toward the room, not into a wall.

Trotting the dog on a treadmill for 20 continuous minutes will give the dog an endurance workout without leaving home. However, it should not be used as a daily replacement for other outside endurance activities.

Training

Treats or toys can be used to train the dog on the treadmill. First reward the dog for getting onto the treadmill while it is turned off. Then, when your dog is not standing on it, turn on the treadmill and reward the dog for standing next to it, to get her familiar with the sound of the treadmill. Start at the slowest possible speed and reward the dog for stepping onto and walking on the treadmill. You may need to hold the treat or toy in front of the dog so that she walks on the treadmill, trying to reach the reward. As she becomes comfortable with the motion of the treadmill, you can gradually increase the speed so that the dog is trotting.

You may need to hold the treat in front of the dog so that the dog walks on the treadmill, trying to reach the reward.

33. Swimming

This low-impact activity is an excellent form of endurance training, and for rehabilitation from muscle or joint injury. The dog should gradually work up to swimming for 10 continuous minutes. If needed, a floating vest can be used to help him stay afloat for an extended period of time.

Training

Use a lightweight lead or leash (at least 6 feet [1.8 meters] long) attached to the dog's buckle collar, to prevent his jumping in and out of the pool. Do not use a slip-lead, which could cause him to become frightened if he feels it tighten around his neck. Depending on how much he enjoys swimming, it may be necessary at first to enter the pool and encourage him gently with the leash to stay in the pool, swimming continuously around in a circle. As the dog becomes familiar with what he is being asked to do, he may only require guidance from a person holding the leash and walking around the pool, while he swims continuously around the periphery of the pool.

Another method of keeping the dog swimming continuously in the pool is to get a toy that floats and toss it toward the center of the pool. As the dog swims back with the toy, take it (or another toy), turn the dog around by gently guiding him by the collar, and toss the toy back out into the pool to retrieve. The dog will be swimming laps with his toy before long.

Swimming is an excellent low-impact exercise that helps a dog retain muscle tone and build aerobic endurance.

Developing Flexibility

Early detection of lumps and other injuries can help diagnose and treat illness or disease. If the dog seems uncomfortable or awkward during a stretch or persists in resisting the stretch, consult your veterinarian to rule out an injury or illness.

GENERAL GUIDELINES FOR PROPER STRETCHING

1. The dog's muscles should be warmed up before stretching—either after a short warm-up walk or after a good workout. Muscles can also be massaged lightly to warm them up for stretching.

2. Both the owner and the dog should be comfortable and relaxed. Sitting on the ground with the dog lying in front is an easy way to do the exercises. Exercises can also be done with small dogs on a sturdy table.

3. The stretch should be a slow, smooth motion.

4. If the dog feels tense, gently massage the area until she relaxes.

5. If there is continued resistance to the stretch, stop and have the dog examined to determine whether there is a physical injury in that area.

Stretching your dog after exercising is important to maintain muscle resilience and flexibility. Stretching promotes good circulation, providing oxygen to overworked parts of the body and improves the range of motion for muscles that move the hind and forelegs.

Stretching also reduces the risk of injury during exercise. Healthy muscles are smooth and stretchy, like rubber bands—they stretch and recover. Once a muscle is torn, it heals, but the scar tissue that forms is not resilient or elastic; the muscle is now more prone to tearing again. Stretching during healing rebuilds and maintains muscle resilience.

An added benefit of participating in stretching exercises with your dog lies in acquiring a greater familiarity with her body.

34. The Play Bow

The play bow is easy to teach and provides a fantastic stretch for the back, neck, forelimbs, and abdominals. It is also a fun trick to impress people with your dog. Begin with the dog in a stand facing you. Hold a tasty treat in front of the dog's nose, to lure her front end back away from you and down. Reward the dog for keeping her elbows on the ground and her head up for the treat. Reward with the treat after the dog holds the bow for 5 seconds, then gradually increase the time to 15 seconds by withholding the treat for longer periods.

step 1

1. Place the dog in front of you in a stand.
2. Lower the treat between the dog's front legs to encourage her to place her elbows on the ground.
3. Once the dog's elbows are on the ground with her head raised, reward her with a tasty treat.

step 2

step 3

The best training treats are small bites of tasty treats that are firm and not crumbly. Large treats will take too long for the dog to eat and he will get full too fast. Crumbly treats end up on the ground and distract the dog from the training. Good examples are cut-up pieces of cheese, hot dog slices, or leftover steak from last night's dinner. All types of cheese are usually delicious to dogs, but mozzarella and string cheese will not melt as quickly in the hand or pocket.

35. Spine Stretches

These exercises give the dog's lower neck, upper thorax, and back a good stretch. Begin with her standing sideways in front of you. Use a tasty treat to lure the dog to reach with her nose along her side, toward her hip. Have the dog hold the position for 5 seconds; reward with the treat and return to the starting position.

Next, use a tasty treat to lure the dog's nose down one of her front legs. Have the dog hold the position for 5 seconds; reward with the treat and return to the starting position.

Finally, use a tasty treat to lure the dog's nose between her front legs. Have the dog hold the position for 5 seconds; reward with the treat. The dog should then train to do this series of reaching and stretching for the treat with her head at all three positions. Begin by having the dog hold each position for a count of 5 seconds; increase to 15 seconds as the dog learns the exercise and becomes more flexible.

step 1

1. Start with the dog in front of you.
2. Use a tasty treat to lure the dog to reach with her nose along her side toward her hip.
3. Lower the dog's nose down the side of her front leg.
4. Lure the dog's nose between her front legs, reaching and stretching for the treat.

step 2

step 3

step 4

36. Chair Stretch

This exercise is an easy and excellent stretch for the dog's back and neck. Use a stool or chair for this exercise. Use a small chair or stool for small dogs and a taller chair for larger breeds. With a tasty treat, lure the dog to put his front feet on the seat of the chair. Have your dog reach up for the treat, keeping his front feet on the chair and his back feet on the ground. Hold the stretch for 5 seconds; gradually increase the duration of the hold for up to 15 seconds by withholding the treat for longer periods.

1. Use a tasty treat to lure the dog to put his front feet on the seat of the chair.
2. With his front feet on the chair, have the dog reach up and stretch for the treat.

step 1

step 2

37. Shoulder Extension

This exercise stretches the large shoulder flexor muscles as well as the elbows. When these muscles tighten, the foreleg may be prevented from extending fully and jumping ability may be compromised. Good range of motion and flexibility can be maintained by stretching these muscles after activity, when they are warm.

Begin with the dog lying on her side. Sit on the side facing the dog's spine. Place one hand on her elbow joint to support it and the other hand in front of her scapula (the shoulder of the top front leg). Gently guide her leg forward while supporting her elbow. Keep her leg parallel to the ground and only stretch the leg as far forward as the dog is comfortable. Move your hand from her elbow to support her wrist, and the hand from her shoulder to support her elbow. Gently guide the leg backward, keeping it parallel to the ground to avoid applying any torque to the joint, and only stretch the leg as far back as is comfortable for the dog. Hold the stretch for 5 seconds, then roll the dog over onto her other side to stretch the other front leg. Increase the holding time to 15 seconds over the course of the next several sessions.

1. Place one hand under the dog's elbow for support and the other on her shoulder, and gently move the foreleg forward to stretch the shoulder and elbow.

2. Move your hand from her elbow to support her wrist, and the hand from her shoulder to support her elbow, and stretch the foreleg further, keeping it parallel to the ground.

step 2

step 1

38. Shoulder Flexion

Flexion is the opposite of extension and is done to maintain balance and resilience. With the dog lying on her side, place one hand on her shoulder and the other hand under the ankle joint of her top front leg. Bring that ankle up to the dog's body. Hold the stretch for 5 seconds, then roll the dog over onto her other side to stretch the other front leg. Increase the holding time to 15 seconds over the course of the next several sessions.

1. Begin with the dog lying on her side. Support the elbow and wrist joint while flexing the front leg up toward the dog's body.

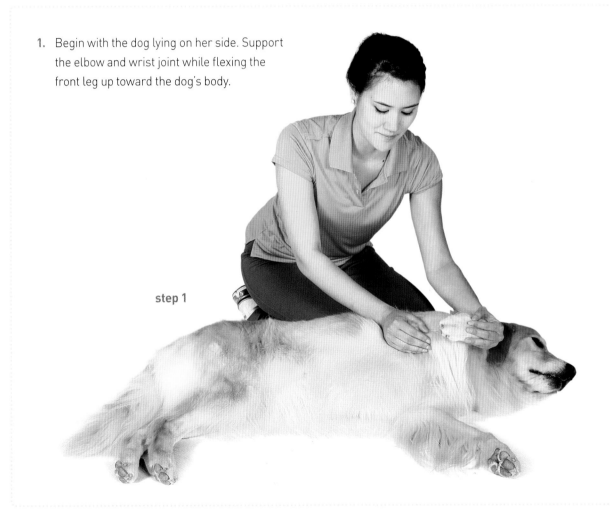

step 1

39. Shoulder Abduction

This exercise stretches the chest and underarm muscles. These muscles work hard in activities that require tight turns (agility, lure coursing) and in weaving (agility).

Begin with the dog lying on her side. Sit on the side facing the dog's spine. Place one hand on the elbow joint of her top front leg and the other hand on the elbow joint of her bottom front leg. Support her elbow joint and press her elbows apart. Only stretch her legs as far apart as the dog is comfortable. Hold the stretch for 5 seconds, then roll the dog over onto her other side to stretch the other front leg. Increase the holding time to 15 seconds over the course of the next several sessions.

1. Begin with the dog lying on her side. Place one hand on the elbow joint of each front leg. Support her elbow joint as you press her elbows apart.

step 1

40. Shoulder Adduction

This exercise, which is the opposite of a shoulder abduction, stretches the large shoulder adductor muscles by bringing the front legs across the midline of the dog's body.

Begin with the dog lying on her side. Sit on the side facing the dog's spine. Place one hand on the elbow joint of her top front leg and the other hand under the elbow joint of her bottom front leg. Support the elbow joints and press the elbows together, crossing the front legs. Only stretch the legs as much as the dog is comfortable. Hold the stretch for 5 seconds, then roll the dog over onto her other side to stretch the other front leg. Increase the holding time to 15 seconds over the course of the next several sessions.

1. Begin with the dog lying on her side. Place one hand on the elbow joint of each front leg. Support her elbow joints as you press his elbows together, crossing her front legs.

step 1

41. Hamstring Stretch

This exercise stretches the hamstring muscles and lower back. Begin with the dog lying on her side. Sit on the side facing the dog's spine. Place one hand on her knee joint and the other hand on the hock joint of her top rear leg. Support her knee joint as you use your other hand to push her leg forward, while supporting the hock joint. Keep her leg parallel to the ground and only stretch the leg as forward as the dog is comfortable. As she becomes more flexible, her rear foot should touch the elbow of her front leg. Hold the stretch for 5 seconds, then roll the dog over onto her other side to stretch the other front leg. Increase the holding time to 15 seconds over the course of the next several sessions.

1. Begin with the dog lying on her side. Place one hand on her knee joint and the other hand on the hock joint of her top rear leg. Support her knee joint as you use your other hand to guide her leg forward, while supporting the hock joint.

step 1

42. Quad Stretch

This exercise stretches the quadriceps and the muscles in the hips and back.

Begin with the dog lying on her side. Sit on the side facing the dog's spine. Place one hand on her knee joint and the other hand on the hock joint of her top rear leg. Support the knee joint and use your other hand to support the hock joint. Push her leg back by applying pressure to the knee joint, straightening the leg back behind the dog. Be sure to support the knee and hock joint during the entire stretch. Keep the leg parallel to the ground and only stretch the leg as backward as the dog is comfortable. As the dog becomes more flexible, the leg should stretch almost straight out behind the dog. Hold the stretch for 5 seconds, then roll the dog over onto her other side to stretch the other front leg. Increase the holding time to 15 seconds over the course of the next several sessions.

1. Begin with the dog lying on her side. Place one hand on the knee joint and your other hand on the hock joint of her top rear leg. Support her knee joint and use your hand on the knee to apply pressure and push the leg back, while supporting the hock joint with your other hand.

step 1

43. Hip Abduction

Begin with the dog lying on her side. Sit on the side facing the dog's spine. Place one hand, palm down, on the inside upper thigh of her lower hind leg. Use the other hand to support her knee and gently press her upper hind leg out from her body. Only stretch the legs as far apart as the dog is comfortable. Hold the stretch for 5 seconds, then roll the dog over onto her other side to stretch the other hind leg. Increase the holding time to 15 seconds over the course of the next several sessions.

step 1

1. Begin with the dog lying on her side. Place one hand on the upper thigh of her bottom hind leg. Support the knee joint of her upper hind leg as you gently press her knees apart.

44. Hip Adduction

Begin with the dog lying on her side. Sit on the side facing the dog's spine. Place one hand on the knee joint of the top hind leg and the other hand under the knee joint of the bottom hind leg. Support her knee joints while gradually bringing her knees together, crossing her hind legs. Only stretch the legs as much as the dog is comfortable. Hold the stretch for 5 seconds, then roll the dog over onto her other side to stretch the other hind leg. Increase the holding time to 15 seconds over the course of the next several sessions.

step 1

1. Begin with the dog lying on her side. Place one hand on the knee joint of each hind leg. Support the knee joints as you bring her knees together, crossing her hind legs.

45. Cat Stretch

The cat stretch stretches the spine and back muscles. Begin with the dog standing. Stand over the dog, facing the same direction. Wrap your arms around the dog's body just behind the front legs and put your hands together under her chest. Lace your fingers together. Starting at her sternum, slowly slide your hands back to the dog's thighs while pulling upward at a 45-degree angle. Do at least three repetitions for a good stretch.

step 1

1. Stand over the dog, facing the same direction. Wrap your arms around the dog's body just behind the front legs and put your hands together under her chest, at her sternum. Lace your fingers together.

2. Begin sliding your hands backward, toward her abdomen.

3. Pull upward at a 45-degree angle as you slide.

4. Continue to slide back, pulling upward, until you reach the dog's hind legs.

step 2

step 4

step 3

46. Pilates Ball Cat Stretch

Using a Pilates ball is fun for dogs and an easy way to stretch the back, spine, and neck muscles. With a tasty treat, lure the dog to place his front feet on the ball, while his back feet remain on the ground. Slowly lower the treat behind the ball until the dog's chest and elbows are on the ball and he is reaching over the ball toward the treat. Hold the stretch for 5 seconds; gradually increase the duration of the hold to 15 seconds by withholding the treat for longer periods.

1. Start with the dog's front feet on the ball. Slowly lower the treat behind the ball until his chest and elbows are on the ball and he is reaching over the ball toward the treat.

step 1

47. Pilates Back and Neck Stretch

This exercise is an easy stretch for the dog's back and neck. With a tasty treat, lure the dog to put his front feet on a Pilates ball. Have him reach upward for the treat, while keeping his front feet on the ball and his back feet on the ground. Have the dog hold the stretch for 5 seconds; gradually increase the duration of the hold to 15 seconds by withholding the treat for longer periods.

1. Start with the dog's front feet on the ball.
2. Slowly raise the treat until he is stretching upward toward the treat, while his front feet remain on the ball and his back feet on the ground.

step 2

step 1

48. Pilates Balance Cushion Stretching

The balance cushion is a great core strengthener because the dog must use her core muscles to balance on the cushion. It is also a great way to get a good stretch of the neck and forelimbs. This stretch is similar to the Chair Stretch (see page 53). Have the dog place her front feet on the balance cushion, while her back feet remain on the ground. As the dog balances, use a treat to lure her to reach upward as far as she can. Hold the stretch for 5 seconds; gradually increase the duration of the hold to 15 seconds by withholding the treat for longer periods.

1. Start with the dog's front feet on the balance cushion.
2. Use a tasty treat to lure her to reach up and stretch without removing her front feet from the balance cushion.

step 1

step 2

Conclusion

Which exercises in Part I did you and your dog enjoy? Make them part of your game plan to achieve your fitness goals. A good way to do this is by making up a weekly chart of exercises and activities. It can be as general as, "Do strengthening exercises today," or as specific as, "5 Sit Ups or Begs + 3 Stand-Down-Stands today."

Having a plan in writing posted on your refrigerator or by the front door is a great way to keep motivated. Post a picture of what you and your dog are working toward. Be proactive and remind yourself daily that fitness is part of your routine now. Your dog and your life depend on getting out and sticking to your plan!

Now move on to Part II for some great ideas on what you can do with your dog—from organized sports to fun activities and games. In addition to describing what is involved in each sport and activity, there are training tips and resources on how to get started. Time, and sometimes financial considerations, are also mentioned, but they are not meant to discourage interest or participation. Commitments are not bad things. Discovering an activity that includes dog and owner as vital parts of a team can unfold into a lifelong passion that extends and enriches both lives.

Sample of a Weekly Fitness Chart

SUNDAY	MONDAY	TUESDAY	WEDNESDAY	THURSDAY	FRIDAY	SATURDAY
Play day	3 Strength Exercises Agility class	30-minute walk, trot, walk (5-20-5)	3 Strength Exercises Agility class	20-minute walk, bike, walk (5-10-5)	3 Strength Exercises Obedience training	Dog park
40-minute beach walk	3 Strength Exercises Agility class	20-minute walk, rollerskate, walk (5-10-5)	3 Strength Exercises Agility class	20-minute walk, trot, walk (5-10-5)	3 Strength Exercises Obedience training	Fun hike

Remember to stretch every day!

PART II

SPORTS
&
GAMES

Playing Organized Sports

Organized dog sports are a fun and exciting way to get out of the house and get in shape with the dog. There are many sports to choose from. In deciding upon a sport, it is important to consider several things.

- Choose something that the dog seems to enjoy or do well. For example, if he does not enjoy retrieving, then a sport such as flyball may not be right for him. But if the dog loves pulling on the leash, a sport such as canicross or skijoring might be just the ticket.

- Choosing an activity for which there already are clubs that sanction and provide training for the sport can make getting started easier.

- Consider how much time is available to train for the sport. Some sports are more time-consuming and require daily training and continuous practicing, whereas others, once trained, take little extra practice time. For example, canicross is based more on the dog's fitness and natural pulling ability, and keeping the dog in shape is the main

concern. On the other hand, agility takes initial training, natural ability, constant practice for course handling, and keeping the dog physically fit for the sport.

- Some sports are more expensive than others. Some can be costly because of the price of equipment, lessons, travel, and entry fees; others require little or no financial outlay. Canicross, for example, has very little cost as compared to herding. Canicross equipment is a harness and lead, it requires no more than basic obedience training, and the only cost would be entry fees for competition. Herding is a sport that takes many lessons and training; lessons and entry fees are expensive because of the livestock involved, and training and practice is ongoing for the entire herding career of the dog.

49. Agility

Canine agility is an exciting sport that offers lots of opportunities to play, exercise, and bond with your dog. In agility, the owner/handler moves with the dog, directing him through a predetermined sequence of obstacles that the dog has been trained to perform. Physically fit dogs and owners excel in this fast-paced, exhilarating sport.

Agility requires a commitment to training, but as with all good things, the journey is its own reward. Positive motivational techniques use rewards, such as toys or treats, to motivate the dog to enjoy performing the obstacles and playing the game with his owner. Positive training methods, such as *clicker training* and *target training*, are used to help the dogs learn to perform the obstacles correctly and safely.

What Makes a Good Agility Dog?

All breeds of dogs, including mixed breeds, are able to learn and compete in agility. Dogs have been bred throughout the years to do specific jobs—retrievers and hounds for hunting, collies and cattle dogs to move stock, terriers for vermin control, and so on. They have been selectively bred for certain physical characteristics to fulfill those jobs.

Agility training provides good physical and mental exercise for both dog and owner. Positive training techniques emphasize *having fun* to motivate dogs to do their best.

Although any dog can be successful in navigating the courses, small- to medium-size breeds excel at agility. Border Collies are found at the top tiers of competition because of their ability to focus, their quickness in response to cues, and their amazing athleticism. Giant breeds may have a difficult time maneuvering on/through/over the equipment, but many nevertheless enjoy the activity.

Agility training is easier for dogs that are food and/or toy motivated. Dogs that are motivated to do whatever they need to do to get a food treat, retrieve a ball, or tug on a toy excel at learning agility. A fit, athletic dog can be trained for longer periods of time and, consequently, learn the game more quickly. Physically fit dogs, especially with regard to their weight, are also able to avoid injuries during training and competition. Dogs that can focus their attention on their owners and who are not easily distracted also excel at agility. Having some basic obedience training —a *stay* command and a reliable *recall*—will help greatly when teaching the obstacles. (See Resources and References, page 166, for how to find a training center or agility training classes.)

Agility classes for beginners usually meet weekly. Small class size, positive training techniques, and instructors who emphasize fun and games are what to look for in a good beginner's class. Class members usually advance as a group to the next level of instruction. Advanced competitors look for instructors who can address particular

Classes for beginners introduce each piece of equipment slowly at lowered heights and offer lots of positive reinforcement for accomplishing each small step successfully. This builds confidence in dogs and emphasizes that agility is fun and rewarding.

Early training on a balance board gets dogs used to movement under their feet. This familiarity is important before introducing the teeter. Dogs must confidently approach the teeter, mount it, tip it, stride into the contact zone, and exit after the board touches the ground.

problems in training (e.g., contacts, course strategy, and so on) either in weekly class meetings or by attending a seminar or taking a private lesson. Agility seminars focus on specific topics over one or two days and are conducted by top-tier competitors and trainers.

50. Agility Obstacles

There are many different training methods in agility for both the handler and the dog. Training can begin with focused attention activities, flatwork exercises, and relationship building. The success of any particular training method depends on the suitability and sensibility of both the handler and the dog. No matter which training method is used, the dog must master the performance of all the agility obstacles.

CONTACT OBSTACLES: A-FRAME, DOG WALK, TEETER TOTTER

Contact obstacles are apparatuses that require dogs to run across or up and over them. The three contact obstacles are the **A-Frame**, **Dog Walk**, and **Teeter Totter**. Each contact obstacle has a contact zone at each end of the obstacle, identified by a contrasting color. In competition, the dog must place at least one paw in the down-side contact zone when exiting the obstacle. Some venues require the dog to place at least one paw in the up-side contact zone when starting the obstacle. The teeter board must hit the ground and the dog must be in the contact zone before exiting. Rules regarding contact obstacles were established to ensure the dog's safety.

Considerations in Starting Agility

- Fitness level of the dog and the handler. The dog must be able to jump, climb, and turn while running. The handler must be able to keep up with the dog, running and turning quickly (crosses).
- Time for training. Ten to 15 minutes of training daily are needed to make good progress in training agility.
- Tasty treats and fun toys. Both are needed for motivation.
- Positive attitude. The handler must keep it fun for the dog.

Dogs with the following characteristics excel at agility:

- Small- to medium-size breed
- Food and/or toy motivated
- Physically fit, especially with regard to their weight
- Attentive and focused on their owner; not easily distracted

The most common top breeds in agility competitions are Border Collies, mixed breeds, Australian Shepherds, Shetland Sheepdogs, Golden Retrievers, Labrador Retrievers, and Jack Russell Terriers. The Teacup Dog Agility Association also includes Papillons, Pembroke Welsh Corgis, and Yorkshire Terriers.

TEACHING OBSTACLES

Begin teaching the contact obstacles by getting the dog familiar with running across low elevated boards and balancing on a balance board. These exercises will give the dog confidence when training on the actual agility obstacles. Teaching the dog to place her feet in the contact zones consistently can be very challenging. It requires the dog to run to the bottom of an incline while in a highly charged state, with the handler running alongside or in front. The longer the dog's stride, the more difficult she is to train, because it is more likely she will stride or jump over the contact zone.

There are several methods for teaching the dog to touch the contact zones. All are food or toy motivated. The best methods are those that teach the dog to work the contacts independently, so the handler can get to the next position.

In the **two-on, two-off method**, the dog is taught to wait at the bottom of the

contact zone with his front feet on the ground and back feet on the obstacle. Most trainers teach the dog to do this by having him go to a target at the bottom of the obstacle, where he is rewarded for waiting in the two-on, two-off position.

Running contacts require the dog to run over the contact without slowing down and purposefully hitting the contact zone. This can be a more difficult method to teach. The dog must learn to use the correct number of strides to land in the contact zone before exiting the obstacle. The dog is rewarded for the performance of the obstacle as he exits the obstacle, usually with a thrown toy or treat bag.

Dogs need a straight approach to run up the A-frame, over the top, and into the contact zone before exiting. One method of training a proper exit off any contact obstacle is the *two-on, two-off* method.

Running contacts require handlers to plan carefully ahead—to be ready to indicate the next obstacle or sequence as the dog hits the contact zone.

51. Herding

The ability to herd livestock is an instinctual ability that has been selectively bred into specific breeds of dogs. Although working livestock is not for all dog breeds, a number of breeds are capable of doing the work. There are many herding breeds, ranging from Border Collies to Corgis. Any herding breed or herding breed mix that has demonstrated herding instinct can learn to work livestock. Herding is an instinctual trait that the dog must be born with to accomplish the task of working livestock. The organizations that offer herding competitions vary on which breeds or mixed breeds are allowed to compete, so it is a good idea to check each organization's rule book.

Defining traits in the different herding breeds were selectively bred into the line for the dog to do a specific job. For example, the Welsh Pembroke Corgi was bred to drive cattle down alleyways and chutes; the dogs' short legs allow them to duck easily below the flying hooves of kicking cattle and their pushy attitude makes it easy for them to move large livestock even where the animals don't want to go. German Shepherds and Briards were bred to work a boundary line to keep the stock grazing in a specific area. Border Collies can work long distances away from their handler (even out of sight) to find and bring back a flock of sheep. Although each breed was bred for a

Working cattle can be very exciting but also dangerous. Cattle can kick and fight with dogs. The dog must be quick on his feet and grip low at the heel to move them.

When fetching stock, the dog goes out and gathers and brings the stock to the handler. Many competitions use different gregarious livestock such as geese, ducks, sheep, goats, and cattle.

Examples of Herding Breeds

Australian Cattle Dog
Australian Shepherd
Bearded Collie
Beauceron
Belgian Malinois
Belgian Sheepdog
Belgian Tervuren
Border Collie
Bouvier des Flandres
Briard
Canaan Dog
Cardigan Welsh Corgi
Collie
German Shepherd
Norwegian Buhund
Old English Sheepdog
Pembroke Welsh Corgi
Polish Lowland Sheepdog
Puli
Pyrenean Shepherd
Shetland Sheepdog
Swedish Vulhund

specific herding job, many can be trained to do more, crossing over to being an all-around ranch dog.

Although each organization has different courses and rules for different levels of herding competition, there are some similarities. Competition at the beginner's level usually demonstrates the dog's ability to control the livestock and to balance and keep the livestock moving *toward* the handler, a natural instinct in stock dogs. At more advanced levels of competition, the handler must take the dog's natural abilities and shape them so that the dog is able to not only bring the stock but also drive the stock *away* from the handler, through gates and obstacles. The higher the level of competition, the farther away the dog must work from the handler to move the stock through the course.

Getting Started in Herding

Many herding organizations around the world offer competitions, such as the American Kennel Club, the International Sheepdog Society, or the West Australian Working Sheepdog Association. Learn about other national and international clubs starting on page 166.

Not all herding dogs still have the natural ability to work stock. The best way to get started is to find a club or training center that offers instinct testing for stock work.

The dog will be put in a pen with sheep and will be tested on his interest and ability to work livestock. If the dog is eager to work and shows some natural instinct, then working livestock is an excellent way to exercise the dog and the handler.

In advanced competitions, dogs drive sheep through obstacles.

52. Obedience

Competitive obedience takes obedience training to its highest level. Dogs that participate in competitive obedience demonstrate a high level of handler-focused attention. They are trained to do heeling, recalls, retrieves, and other exercises with pinpoint accuracy. Refining a dog's skills and behaviors can be fun to train and a pleasure to watch.

Dogs that excel in obedience competition come from many different breeds, including mixed breeds. In advanced levels of competition, they must be able to jump over a bar set at shoulder height and to jump a broad jump with a spread twice the height of the jump bar. Dogs must be at least six months old to begin competing in obedience trials.

Example of heeling work

Example of retrieve over
high jump exercise

Several organizations offer obedience competition and titling (see page 166). They require the completion of similar exercises to earn qualifying scores for titles. Points are deducted for less than perfect execution of the exercises, including out-of-position sitting (in front or at the side) or heeling (lagging or forging ahead), the handler's giving multiple commands, or the dog's failing to do the exercise.

Novice level competition usually involves heeling on leash (including halts, turns, and changes in pace), examination by a judge, recall, and long sit and down.

At more advanced levels of competition, the dog must be able to perform a broad jump, retrieve a dumbbell, drop on command during a recall, and stay in a long sit and long down with the handler out of sight.

Signal exercises (only hand signals are used), scent discrimination (finding an article with the handler's scent on it), directed retrieves, moving stand and exam, and directed jumping are required exercises at the top levels of competition.

When trained with positive motivation, all of the competitive obedience exercises can be enjoyable as well as challenging to train and perform for both dog and handler. Most trainers use clicker training and other positive reinforcement methods to increase the dog's enjoyment in performing the exercises. A well-trained, enthusiastic dog working in tandem with his handler is a joy to watch in competitive obedience.

Getting Started in Obedience

There are many books on obedience training that can help teach the exercises with positive training methods. Check for a local obedience club in your area (see page 166) by visiting the organizations' websites.

Example of scent discrimination exercise

53. Canine Freestyle

Simply stated, canine freestyle is dancing with dogs to music. On a competitive level, canine freestyle is a modern dog sport that combines the perfection of obedience with the athleticism, tricks, rhythm, and creativity of dance, into a routine that showcases the strong bond between dog and handler. Competition is open to all breeds and mixed breeds. Focused attention, good overall fitness, and intelligence are required for dogs to compete in canine freestyle.

There are two main types of canine freestyle: *musical freestyle* and *freestyle heeling* (heelwork to music). In freestyle heeling, the dog and handler stay close together, "moving as one" through pivots, backward, forward, and sideways, in time to a chosen musical

Canine Freestyle teams incorporate showmanship and elaborate costumes when they compete.

SEE SPOT RUN

selection. Nonheeling activities (jumping, weaving, rolling, and passing through the owner's legs) are not allowed.

In musical freestyle, heelwork can be combined with tricks such as leg weaving, rolling over, turns, bows, sending out and moving with each other, and even jumping into the handler's arms. Innovative tricks done as dance moves are encouraged. Greater focus is placed on the handler's creativity in matching the team's actions with the music.

Training Tips

- Use toys and treats and lots of praise when the dog does the behavior you want to train.

- Patie Ventre, founder of the World Canine Freestyle Organization (WCFO), uses a clicker *after* the dog has learned the correct behavior, to perfect the move and to train for consistency.

- Train each movement separately, not as part of a dance.

- Each dog has dance moves that he likes to perform. A good team capitalizes on these moves and uses them to enhance the performance.

Getting Started in Freestyle

To begin, find a good obedience class that will teach your dog the basic commands, and more important, teach him to pay close attention to you (focused attention). Also, attend a local canine event where you can meet people who are involved in canine freestyle. Attending a seminar or conference can provide a lot of

training information and insight in a short period of time.

Various organizations also offer titling tests, which represent the standards they have set for different levels of expertise. The dog/handler teams either pass the test or retry them at a later date. WCFO proficiency tests at the bronze bar level (beginner) are open to everyone, including nonmembers.

Several organizations regulate competitive freestyle, including the World Canine Freestyle Organization (WCFO), the Canine Freestyle Federation (CFF), and the Musical Dog Sport Association (MDSA) in the United States; Paws 2 Dance Canine Freestyle Organization in Canada; and Canine Freestyle GB (Great Britain) and Pawfect K9 Freestyle Club (Japan) internationally.

Competition rules vary among organizations and from country to country, but most judging is based on accumulating merit points. Single dog-and-handler teams, a pair of dogs with one handler (called a *brace*), or teams of three or more dogs and handlers are judged on technical and artistic points, much like competitive figure skating. Some organizations place a greater emphasis on dance choreography and costumes (showmanship), whereas others emphasize the athleticism and skills of the dog and the partner's ability to handle the dog.

Look into these organizations by visiting their websites (see page 166), to find the one that best suits your needs or to locate a club or training facility in your area. If you can't find one in your area, order an instructional DVD from an association specializing in this activity.

54. Rally

Rally is an excellent starting point for anyone interested in entering the world of canine competition. The exercises are fun to teach, using positive reinforcement techniques, and can help the dog move on to other areas of competition. Rally encourages communication and teamwork between dog and handler. It can help improve the bond between dogs and their owner.

Although rally obedience is not an aerobic activity for the owner or the dog, it does involve getting out and moving with the dog, joining training classes, and stimulating the mind. Rally is a low-impact exercise that is good for all dogs, including older dogs, and good for all humans, including older humans and even those who are physically handicapped. Rally competition, like obedience competition, can be done from an electric wheelchair.

In rally, dogs and their handler must complete a course of ten to twenty stations (depending on the level of competition), each with a sign stating a skill to be performed. They include descriptions as well as directional arrows. The signs are numbered and must be performed sequentially. Handlers are given a chance to walk the course together to familiarize themselves with the signs and sequence before their turn to run. They may also question the judge about the signs. Once they are instructed by the judge to begin their run, the dog-and-handler team moves at its own pace, with the dog on a loose leash on the handler's left side. Communication between handler and dog is encouraged—including talking, praising, clapping hands, patting legs, or any other means of encouragement. Perfect position during heeling is not required.

As in competitive obedience, dogs of all breeds and mixed breeds can excel at rally. Depending on the sponsoring organization, even dogs with physical limitations can compete successfully in rally. The only requirement is that they be at least six months old before entering a trial.

At the novice level of AKC rally competition, all exercises are performed with the dogs on a loose leash. The teams must successfully complete 10 to 15 stations. The handlers may use physical encouragement, such as clapping their hands and patting their legs, throughout the course.

Rally course

At the advanced level, more difficult exercises are performed off-leash. The teams must successfully complete 12 to 17 stations, including having the dogs go over a jump. At the highest level of AKC rally, the handlers may encourage their dogs verbally, but physical encouragement, such as leg patting, is not allowed. The honors exercise requires the dog who completes the course to sit in a designated area close to the finish line until the dog after him has completed his turn.

Getting Started in Rally

As in competitive obedience, many good books describe the signs, exercises, and training techniques for rally. Organizations that sponsor rally trials include the American Kennel Club, Association of Pet Dog Trainers, World Wide Kennel Club, Canadian Kennel Club, and Canadian Association of Rally Obedience (see page 166). Go to their websites to find a trial to attend as a spectator or a club that offers classes in rally.

Training Techniques

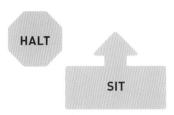

HALT-SIT: While heeling, the handler stops and the dog sits in heel position (on the handler's left side). After a slight pause, the team moves forward with the dog in heel position. This is an example of a *stationary exercise*.

ABOUT TURN: While heeling, the team makes a 180-degree about turn to the handler's right.

RIGHT TURN: The handler and dog make a 90-degree turn to the right.

WEAVE ONCE: The dog and handler move in and out through a line of posts placed 6 to 8 feet (1.8 to 2.4 meters) apart, entering from the left. The dog and handler completes the exercise by passing the last post.

55. Disc Dog

Disc dog is an exciting sport for any dog, regardless of breed or size. Medium-size breeds usually excel at disc dog because of their speed and jumping ability, but any size dog can play the games and have tons of fun. Dogs that compete in disc dog are on the top end of the fitness scale. Success in this sport requires fast acceleration and good catching skills. The dogs must be able to run, jump, and catch for extended periods of time. In addition to having a healthy cardio system, the dogs must be sound in structure. Repetitive jumping and turning places a lot of stress on a dog's hind legs and hips.

In competition, there are several different games to choose from, depending on the dog and handler's abilities and skill levels. Participants can compete in distance and accuracy trials, and freestyle competition. There are also variations, such as the extreme distance challenge and time trials (in distance and accuracy competition); there are individual and pairs freestyle, as well.

Disc dog training and competition does not require the owner to run with the dog, but it does require throwing ability and fitness. In freestyle, the handler must be able to stand, bend, crouch, jump, and throw. Training for competition provides a physical and mental workout for the owner as well as the dog.

In distance and accuracy competition, contestants must throw a disc as many times as possible at a specified distance, within a limited amount of time.

Freestyle is a routine created by the handler, in which the dog performs complicated tricks—vaulting off the handler, jumping, and flipping in the air to catch the disc.

Training for disc dog is fun and rewarding. It provides a great mental and physical workout for high-energy dogs. A dog that loves to retrieve toys is a good candidate for disc dog. Introducing the disc as a toy is best to do when the dog is young, but any dog that likes to retrieve can learn to enjoy the disc as a toy.

Freestyle is an exercise in which the dog performs tricks, vaulting off the handler, jumping, and flipping in the air to retrieve the disc.

Training for Disc Dog

Training for distance and accuracy trials concentrate on teaching the dog to catch the disc while in flight (requires great acceleration and timing), turning quickly, and returning to the handler as fast as possible. The dog's reward can be as simple as another throw. The faster the dog returns with the disc, the faster he gets another chance to chase and retrieve. Teaching the owner how to throw the disc with accuracy and consistency can be the most difficult part of the training! Consistently accurate throws ensure reliable and safe catches by the dog.

Freestyle training and competition requires imagination, concentration, and endurance by both dog and handler. Short, quick tosses; the handling of multiple discs; and body vaults, somersaults, and flips can all be part of a choreographed routine that wows the crowd at every disc dog competition.

Currently, several organizations sponsor disc dog tournaments (see page 166). Most competitions take place in the summer on flat, grassy fields. Fun and safety are major concerns for all organizations.

Disc dog is a growing sport all over the world, and it can be played and trained anywhere, from the beach to the backyard. It is a great way for dogs and their owner to get out and get some exercise.

56. Flyball

Flyball is an active and fun way for dog owners to interact with their dog and other dog enthusiasts in a very stimulating environment. It is a great way to exercise high-drive dogs, and it gets the owners outside training, interacting with people, and builds a strong bond between owners and dogs.

Flyball is a relay in which teams of four dogs race against one another. The dogs run and jump over a line of four hurdles to a box that releases a tennis ball. The ball pops out to be caught when the dog presses a spring-loaded pad. The dog then runs back over the jumps to the handler with the ball.

Flyball

Training for Flyball

Training techniques vary, but training the dog to hit the box with a swimmer's turn and to catch the ball that pops out is the most difficult part. Other training involves getting the dog to ignore the dogs running in the lane beside him and concentrating on the task. Handlers use clickers and toys to train the box, and use toys and tugging to get the dog to run back fast down the lane with the ball. Dogs are rewarded enthusiastically for all work.

The hurdle height is determined by the shoulder height of the smallest dog on the team. Each dog must return its ball across the start line before the next dog can start. Ideally, the dogs will cross nose-to-nose at the start line. The first team to have all four dogs cross the finish line without making a mistake wins the heat. Penalties are applied if the ball is dropped or if the next relay dog is released early. An electronic eye times the dogs and notes if they are released too early. The dogs earn titles and awards based on points earned by their team in racing.

Although competitions may vary, flyball teams are normally assigned to divisions against other teams of similar speed. This allows the races to be closer and much more exciting. Each team in the division races against all the other teams in a round robin format. The team with the most wins is the overall winner.

Flyball competition is open to all breeds of dogs, including mixed breeds. This is part of its great popularity as a dog sport. Although Border Collies and terriers excel at flyball, any dog that loves to retrieve tennis balls can get into the game. Any size dog is acceptable. Teams almost always have one short dog on the team, called a *height dog*, because the height of the smallest dog on the team determines the height of the hurdles the team will jump. Small dogs' only limitation is their ability to press the trigger on the flyball box to release the ball. They are even allowed to use smaller-size tennis balls.

Getting Started in Flyball

There are two flyball organizations in the United States: the North American Flyball Association (NAFA) and the more recently established United Flyball League International (UFLI). The main flyball organization in Great Britain is the British Flyball Association (BFA), and in Australia, the Australian Flyball Association (AFA). Flyball is also very popular in Canada. The Canadian Kennel Club (CKC) is a sanctioning organization for flyball tournaments and titling.

To locate a dog club or flyball club near you or to find local tournaments to attend, see page 166.

57. Scent Hurdles

Scent hurdle racing is a fun sport that uses a dog's speed and ability to quickly distinguish scents, as well as his ability to jump. Although any athletic dog can participate successfully in this sport, terriers and Border Collies excel in this game. The smallest dog on the team determines the jump height for that team, so most teams include a small, fast dog. Scent hurdle racing is popular throughout Europe and Canada. The Canadian Kennel Club has a titling program in scent hurdles.

Scent hurdle races are run much like flyball races, except that the dog retrieves a scented dumbbell instead of a tennis ball. Scent hurdle races are made up of two teams of four handlers and their dogs, plus a platform steward. Both teams race their dogs side by side in relay style, over a series of four hurdles. The jump height for each team is determined by the smallest dog running in each heat. Each dog retrieves his handler's naturally scented dumbbell, and returns immediately back over the hurdles to his handler. The successive dogs are sent to repeat the same performance, until the last dog on the team has completed his run. The first team to successfully complete the course is the winner of that heat. The first team to win two out of three heats is the winner of the race.

Teaching a dog to run down the line over the hurdles is not difficult, but it can sometimes be challenging during competition when there is the additional excitement of other dogs running close by. Dogs will sometimes leave their racing lane and return over the hurdles in another lane.

Training for scent discrimination with dumbbells is done in the same manner as in obedience training. The dog is rewarded for choosing the dumbbell that has the owner's scent on it. Other dumbbells are introduced with the scented dumbbell; the dog is rewarded when he chooses the correct dumbbell. Training is not difficult but must be thorough for the dog to be able to do it quickly in the highly charged atmosphere of scent hurdle racing.

Getting Started in Scent Hurdles

Look for a flyball or scent hurdle team in your area. The Canadian Kennel Club lists local clubs with scent hurdle racing and flyball teams (see page 166).

A dog's sense of smell is amazing. They can follow a trail and discriminate between scents easily.

58. K9 Nose Work

K9 nose work was inspired by the training methods of detection canines. K9 nose work defines this detection-inspired sport that has evolved from the pursuit of dogs and their handlers to practice nose work and have fun.

Any breed of dog as well as mixed breeds can participate in K9 nose work. Dogs must prequalify for titling trials by passing an Odor Recognition Test (ORT). The test requires the dog to identify a box scented with a particular scent (which depends on the level of titling—birch, anise, or clove) from a lineup of at least twelve and up to twenty boxes, each of which contains no other distracting odors. The purpose of the ORT is to show that the dog recognizes the odor that will be used in the titling trial. The dog has three minutes to alert (signal) the handler that it has found the correct scented box. The dog may then proceed on to the titling exercise.

Titling trials include a box drill, exterior search, interior search, and vehicle search for the identified odor (birch, anise, or clove). Each element is assigned a point value, the sum of all the elements adding up to 100 points. Placements during nose work competition are based on the team's cumulative score. There is also a maximum time limit per element, which cannot be exceeded if points are to be awarded. The elements may be presented in any order. Advanced titling challenges the dog's ability to detect the odor under increasingly difficult conditions, for example, by adding various shapes and distracting odors to the box drill, selecting outdoor areas with a multitude of distractions, working in inclement weather and wind conditions, increasing the size of the interior search area (one to four rooms), or movement of the odor within and among selected vehicles.

Getting Started in Nose Work

The National Association of Canine Scent Work (NACSW) provides a list of certified instructors in scent work (see page 166) as well as a trialing calendar.

A dog taking the Odor Recognition Test (ORT) in order to qualify for a titling trial

59. Tracking

Tracking is a true team sport between human and dog. It provides an excellent means of exercise for both the owner and the dog, while utilizing the dog's natural ability for scent work.

Any breed or mixed breed dog can track. Although scent hounds are famous for the ability to use their nose, any dog is capable of learning to track. Training can begin at any age; even an eight-week-old puppy can begin learning nose work using positive reinforcement techniques.

In tracking, the dog finds a track laid by a *track layer* and follows its scent to find an article left by the track layer. The handler's job is to recognize that the dog is on the track and following the right scent. The dog is the leader of the team, remaining out in front on a long lead, while the handler supports the dog without impeding his progress.

Dogs' sense of smell is amazing. Dogs are able to tell the difference between tracks that were made at different times, even if they cross one another. They are able to follow tracks that are hours old and that animals or other humans have crossed over since. Once the dog learns to follow the scent that he is shown, he will follow it no matter what its age, the surface it is on, or how many other tracks have crossed it.

The beginning of the track is marked with a flag. The handler follows the dog once the dog has gone to the end of the tracking line to follow the scent.

Track Odors

Five types of scent are available to the dog to distinguish the track. Four are part of the track, and a fifth is on and near the article left behind by the track layer.

1. The first scent is made up of particles of human skin floating in the air near the track. The position of these particles can change, depending on wind conditions, but in general, the particles' scent will not be detectable 10 to 15 feet (3 to 4.6 meters) from either side of the walker's path.

2. The second type of scent is the smell of crushed vegetation. Damaged leaves and stems give off an odor much as a freshly mowed lawn does. Each footprint made by the track layer creates a crushed vegetation scent that the dog can follow. The scent of crushed vegetation can last a long time.

3. The third scent for the dog to follow is the scent of disturbed soil. Microbes in soil let out gas particles that, when disturbed, give the earth a strong odor.

4. The fourth scent is the smell from the particles that are rubbed off from the track layer's shoes. Although this scent is not usually a strong one, it is available to the dog as a way to recognize the track it is following.

5. The fifth scent comes from the article left behind by the track layer. The scent comes from the material and the personal odor transferred to it by the track layer. The scent of the article can be spread out by the wind and air currents over a wide area.

Training for Tracking

The equipment needed for training includes a harness for the dog, a 40-foot (12-meter) tracking long line, eight to twelve surveyor's flags or other type of flags to mark a track, training treats such as sliced hot dogs, articles to leave behind (an old leather glove or cotton sock), and a journal for recording tracks laid.

Training is done with treat motivation —all positive motivation with no negative corrections given to the dog. The dog finds treats along the track as a reward for following the track. Lots of treats are used to lay the track at the beginning of the training, but are gradually reduced as the dog becomes better at following the track. The dog also gets a substantial reward when he finds the article left by the track layer.

Getting Started in Tracking

The American Kennel Club, Australian Shepherd Club of America (ASCA), and United Kennel Club (UKC) all have titling programs in tracking. Check their websites for more information about their tracking programs (see page 166).

60. Dock Diving

Any dog that loves to jump, retrieve, and be in water can participate in dock diving. The organizations that promote dock diving competitions allow mixed breeds as well as pure breeds. No size limitation exists in dock diving—there's a class for small dogs; other classes are divided up by how far the dogs can jump. There are two types of competitions: *distance competition,* which primarily measures horizontal distance, and *super-vertical* or *extreme-vertical* competition.

In distance competition, the dogs run down a 36-foot (11 meter) dock elevated 2 feet (0.6 meter) above the surface of the pool. The pool is 40 feet (12.2 meters) long. Dogs are entered in heats, called *waves.* The dogs are allowed two jumps per wave. The dogs run down the dock and leap into the pool for a thrown toy. The distance the dog jumps is measured from the end of the dock to where the dog's rump hits the water. Each dive is measured to determine the winner of each wave. The dog with the longest jump wins the wave. The top twenty-four longest dives from all the waves compete in a finals round against one another.

In super vertical or extreme vertical, a bumper toy is suspended 8 feet (2.4 meters) from the dock and at least 4 feet 6 inches (1.4 meters) above the dock. It is raised in 2-inch (5 cm) increments. Competitors may enter their dog at any height. Dogs are allowed two attempts to pull the bumper off the clips.

Getting Started in Dock Diving

The four organizations that promote the sport of dock diving are Splash Dogs, Dock Dogs, Ultimate Air Dogs (UKC titling), and the Super Retriever Series. (See page 166 for website information.)

Six Levels of Distance Competition

JUNIOR HANDLER	for any handler younger than 16 years of age
LAP DOG	for dogs less than 12 inches (30.5 cm) high at the withers (shoulders)
SPLASH CLASS	dogs jump to 9 feet 11 inches (just under 3 meters)
JUNIOR CLASS	dogs jump from 10 feet to 14 feet 11 inches (3 to 4.5 meters)
SENIOR CLASS	dogs jump from 15 feet to 19 feet 11 inches (4.6 to 6 meters)
PRO	dogs jump from 20 feet to 23 feet 11 inches (6.1 to 7.25 meters)
EXTREME	dogs jump 24 feet (7.3 meters) or more

Training for Dock Diving

Finding a place to train can be the most challenging aspect of dock diving. It is not easy to find a dock and body of water long enough to train in. Practice runs are offered before wave competition begins, sometimes for a fee. Many people who do not have access to training are only able to train at the competitions.

There are two training methods/ strategies for dock diving. In *place and send*, the handler throws the toy into the pool, takes the dog back up the dock, and releases her to run down the dock and jump into the pool for the toy. This method is common with beginners. More experienced competitors use a *chase* method, whereby the dog is placed in a sit or down-stay at the head of the dock. The handler goes to the end of the dock, calls the dog, and throws the toy into the air as she jumps for the toy out over the water. Either method is accepted in competition. What works best for the dog to get the longest jump is what competitors are looking for.

In all organizations, the dog must jump on her own accord; she cannot be thrown into the water. The main goal for all dock diving competitions is for the dogs and owners to have fun.

Distance competition

Super-vertical competition

61. Draft Work (Carting)

Dogs traditionally bred to pull carts loaded with milk cans, farm produce, or small children excel at this gentle sport due in large part to their physical strength and sound temperaments. Draft work, or "carting," is a centuries-old tradition with such breeds as Bernese Mountain Dogs, Swiss Mountain Dogs, Newfoundlands, collies, Bouviers, and Saint Bernards. Titling in this sport can only be accomplished through one of these breed clubs (see page 166). All clubs welcome all breeds, including mixed breeds, to participate and earn draft dog titles. Titling requirements vary among clubs, but not to a great degree.

A physically fit dog is of paramount importance in beginning draft work. The dog must be orthopedically sound with no indication of structural or gaiting problems. Just as important is the dog's temperament. He must be comfortable working through noisy distractions and not be prone to startling, remaining focused on the job at hand and attentive to his handler. Dogs must be able to walk on a loose leash, stay, and come when called.

Getting Started

Visit the website for one of the breed clubs to find a local club to contact. Club members who participate in draft work are usually passionate about their sport. They will be able to give advice on how to be fitted correctly for a harness, where to get an appropriate harness, and how to proceed with training. (See page 166.)

A dog pulls a weighted cart during the half-mile (0.8 km) freight haul.

Carting course

Draft Tests

To pass a draft test:

1. The dog must first demonstrate the ability to follow basic commands from his handler: forward, halts, change of pace (fast, slow), turning about, and coming when called.

2. The dog and handler must then maneuver through a course, which includes a station to hitch up the cart, making right and left turns, circling right and left, adding a load onto the cart, unloading the load, being greeted by a stranger, backing up, working through visual and audio distractions, slowing down the pace, passing through a narrow area, and waiting until an obstacle is removed from the dog's path. The exercises are done at the novice level on a loose leash and off-leash (the dog must keep within an arm's length from the handler) at the open level.

3. The dog must also stay in the ring with other dogs in a stand, sit, or down, with their carts attached, for 3 minutes while their respective handlers stand across the ring for novice, or out of sight in open.

4. The final exercise in the draft test is the ½-mile (0.8 kilometer) freight haul, during which the teams demonstrate their ability to pull and control a weighted cart over the natural terrain of the area (ideally, this includes uphill and downhill slopes and changes in footing).

Note: the above guidelines are those of the Bernese Mountain Dog Club of America, though your home country or region's guidelines may differ.

Training

Training is done with lots of treats and praise at every step. The dog is always kept on leash during his training, for the handler to be able to control his response and avoid potentially dangerous situations. Training starts with introducing the harness. After the dog is comfortable wearing the harness around the house and on walks, traces (straps that attach the harness to the cart) are added to get the dog used to them dragging along his body. The dog is treated and praised for walking without being distracted by the traces. When the dog is comfortable with that stage, light weights (light pieces of wood or plastic milk bottles filled with some sand) are added to the ends of the traces. Care and patience must be taken at every step to ensure the dog's success during training.

The dog must be thoroughly familiar with the cart and comfortable walking alongside it and between the shafts, before he is hitched up to it. Carts can make odd noises that may take getting used to. Treat and feed around the cart to ensure a positive association with it. Some dogs are bothered by having something following closely behind them. Patience and an upbeat attitude will greatly aid in training the dog for draft work.

62. Weight Pulling

The sport of weight pulling is currently enjoyed by dogs of all breeds and mixed breeds. No longer dominated by freight dogs such as the Alaskan Malamutes, the sport now includes large breeds such as mastiffs, Saint Bernards, and Newfoundlands; mid-sized bully breeds such as boxers and pit bulls; and small breeds such as terriers and toy poodles. They include dogs that have been bred to pull and dogs that just love to pull.

The dogs pull wheeled carts on dirt or rail tracks, or sleds on snow. The track is 10 feet wide by 16 feet long (3 by 4.9 meters). The dog must pull the cart the length of the track upon a verbal command from her handler, who stands at the finish line. Once the handler calls the dog, she must complete the pull within a set period of time, usually 60 seconds. The handler can encourage the dog verbally, but cannot touch the dog or cart, or use food or toys to lure her.

Every dog starts her heat with the same weight, usually the weight of the cart. The weight is increased in increments. The dog can move on to the next weight level if she pulls the cart the length of the track in the required length of time. The dogs then compete against

This dog won a weight-pull competition at a state fair by pulling 1,880 pounds (853 kg) during his very first competition.

other dogs in their own weight class. The dog that pulls the most amount of weight successfully wins her weight class.

Dogs should not pull large amounts of weight nor train or compete in this activity before they are eighteen months old. Pulling very heavy weights before their growth plates have closed can have serious long-term effects on joint development in young dogs.

Training Tips

- Do not begin training or competing young dogs before their growth plates have closed (usually after 18 months of age).
- Allow the dog to wear the harness around the house while receiving lots of praise and treats.
- When the dog is comfortable with the harness, attach empty plastic jugs to the harness, then add weight gradually by pouring gravel inside the jugs.
- Dogs have to get used to the noise of the cart and the presence of something following closely behind them. Proceed slowly when introducing the cart. Avoid a negative experience for the dog by using lots of praise and treats, and by keeping the training sessions short.
- Dogs who succeed in this sport *love* to pull. The owner needs only to figure out what best motivates the dog to pull and keep pulling to complete the run.

Training

Training begins with familiarizing the dog with the special harness by having her wear the harness while receiving lots of praise and tasty treats. Weight is added gradually, starting with empty plastic jugs. Gravel is added to make the jugs both heavier and noisier. When the dog is old enough and comfortable pulling weights with the harness, she is introduced to the sled or cart. Obedience training will help the dog focus and follow the handler's commands from a distance.

Handlers must also find out what best motivates their dog to pull, and how to keep her from quitting in the middle of a pull.

Getting Started

The best way to begin is to attend a weight pulling event. The International Weight Pulling Association (IWPA) holds weight pulls for dogs of any breed. They are good places to meet people who are experienced in the sport and who enjoy introducing new people to their sport. They offer a good opportunity to try on a special weight-pulling harness on your dog, and find out if she is inclined naturally to pull heavy weights. (See Resources and References, page 166.)

63. Lure Coursing

Dogs love the thrill of the chase, whether chasing a squirrel or a toy. Lure coursing is a fantastic sport for dogs that love to chase, as it simulates the chase during the hunt. Before lure coursing was invented as a sport, sighthounds hunted live prey, but it was difficult to control the terrain and the prey.

Originally this sport was only open to sighthounds, such as Whippets and Greyhounds. But today, several organizations allow any breed of dog to compete. The sighthounds are still at the pinnacle of the lure coursing world, but many different breeds compete very successfully in this event.

Obstacle lure coursing

Lure coursing

Dogs should be at least one year old to compete. The hard, fast turns can strain a young dog's developing joints. If this occurs repeatedly before the dog's growth plates have closed at eighteen months of age, it can cause serious joint problems later in life.

In lure coursing, the dogs chase an artificial lure across a field, following a pattern that is meant to simulate the live chase. The course must have a minimum number of turns, to mimic the jack rabbit or hare's changing directions during the chase. Sometimes the fields are fenced, but that is not required. The courses are at least 600 yards (0.55 kilometer) long and can be up to 1,000 yards (0.9 kilometer) long.

Course a'Lure

Course a'Lure, a U.S.-based organization owned and operated by Bob and Cyndi Conwell, travels all over the United States and Canada, offering obstacle lure coursing to people and their dogs who wish to give it a try. The dogs are enticed to chase the lure through obstacles such as tires, tunnels, and chutes. The dogs love it and it is a fantastic game for them. Course a'Lure is not a titling organization, but it offers exciting obstacle lure coursing for fun at shows and fairgrounds. See page 166 to learn about Course a'Lure's online events schedule.

Training

Training dogs for lure coursing is usually quite simple, as sight hounds take to it naturally, and many other breeds that have prey drive can be easily encouraged to chase a lure. Training usually begins with a young dog or puppy's chasing a lure on a line. The distance to chase the lure increases as the dog gets older and more enthusiastic.

Getting Started

Begin by contacting a local club, many of which offer training classes and practice sites for lure coursing. There are several organizations that sponsor competitions and titling in lure coursing (See page 166). Only sighthounds listed with the American Sighthound Field Association (ASFA) are eligible to enter their trials; likewise, the American Kennel Club (AKC) only accepts sighthounds that are in AKC's registry. The Fédération Cynologique Internationale (FCI) is a purebred dog organization in Europe that offers titling and competition in lure coursing. The Lure Coursing Fanatics Club (LCFC) is a lure coursing and titling organization that allows all breeds, as well as mixed breeds, to compete. Whether the dog is a Chihuahua or a Great Dane, if he loves to chase things, he is welcome.

64. Go-to-Ground, or Earthdog

Terriers and Dachshunds were originally bred to hunt vermin that live in underground dens. Go-to-Ground or Earthdog competitions demonstrate such breeds' instinct to hunt rodents and tunnel to find them. Competitions gauge the dogs' instinct and their willingness to seek their quarry underground.

Small terriers excel at this competition. Larger terriers were not made for tunneling, so this sport is restricted to the smaller breeds such as fox terriers, West Highland Terriers, rat terriers, Jack Russell Terriers, and Dachshunds. See page 166 for organizations that offer Earthdog or Go-to-Ground titling programs.

While each association has different criteria for their tests, all the clubs test the natural ability of the terrier to find game. The lowest level of testing for every organi-

Training

Getting your dog to follow scent trails of animals is easy. Whenever you see rabbits, squirrels, and other small animals run into the bushes, take him to that area and encourage him to follow the scent trail left by the animal. Build tunnels at home, either with wooden boxes placed underground or above ground, or with cardboard boxes in the house. These activities will help your dog feel comfortable about going out of your sight and into dark places in search of the prey.

Training the dog to follow a scent trail is not difficult. If you do not have rats to mark the trail and wait in a cage at the end of the tunnel, ask someone at a local pet shop to give you some used bedding after they clean the rodent cages. Put the bedding in a sock and soak it in water. Use the strained liquid to lay trails in the tunnels for the dog.

Earthdog competitions measure a dog's instinct and willingness to hunt prey underground.

zation is an instinct test. This test looks for natural behaviors in the dog. The dog is tested on his ability to follow a scent to the entrance of a tunnel and his willingness to enter a dark den and work the quarry. The judges want to see the dog barking, digging, growling, lunging, and biting at the protective cage with the rats in it, to gauge his desire to get the quarry. In more advanced tests, the dog must follow longer scent trails and go through a maze of underground tunnels to get to the quarry. The prey are always kept in a cage, safe from the dog.

Getting Started

The best way to find out if your dog has a strong prey drive is to go to an Earthdog test or practice. Contact an organization that holds Earthdog or Go-to-Ground tests, and get a schedule of events for your area. Visit each organization's website (see page 166) for rules and regulations, and decide which best suits your needs. Get the organization's rule book —knowing the rules and what the dog needs to do to qualify in a test is the first step toward entering a competition.

Earthdog tunnel construction

65. Field Trials and Hunt Tests

Through the ages, dogs have been used to help people hunt many kinds of wild animals, from lions and wild boar to elk and partridges. It was the first form of work for domesticated dogs. Hunt tests and field trials showcase the close relationship between hunting dogs and their owners.

The differences between field trials and hunt tests vary among different organizations. On a very basic level, dog and handler teams compete against each other for points at field trials and compete against defined skill standards during a hunt test.

Field trials are made up of different competitions (*stakes*) within the trial. Depending on the dog breed club hosting the trial, a trial may require retrieving downed waterfowl or pointing out game birds. Handlers work from the ground or on horseback. Dog and handler teams accumulate points based on their performance, which determine placements (first through fourth place).

Dogs are judged against a breed standard in hunt tests. The skills being tested vary

Field trial

according to the dog's breed—the dog is tested to see how well they can do what he was bred to do.

Field trials and hunt tests are almost exclusively attended by sporting dogs or gun dogs—dogs bred to hunt birds. They include retrievers, pointers, spaniels, and setters. These breeds have been developed to specialize in specific hunting tasks—pointers point, spaniels flush out game, and retrievers bring back the downed bird. Field trials and hunt tests, and the training involved, allow these dogs to use their skills and instincts to do the jobs they were born to do.

Getting Started

The best way to begin in this sport is to find a mentor with experience in training your dog's breed or a similar breed. It is also a good idea to visit the different organizations' websites to determine which type of competition best suits you and your dog. Breed-specific hunting clubs are also a good source of information to get you started.

The Amateur Field Trial Clubs of America (AFTCA) is considered to offer the highest level of field trialing, but does not do titling. The North American Versatile Hunting Dog Association (NAVHDA), also considered a high-level venue, sanctions hunt tests and does titling. The American Kennel Club (AKC) sanctions both hunt tests and field trials and awards titles to both hunt-tested dogs and field trial dogs. The United Kennel Club (UKC) sanctions hunt tests and field trials for bird dogs and other hunting dogs and offers titling as well. (See page 166.)

Training

As with other sports and activities that involve some amount of instinct (herding or tracking), training for field work varies greatly, depending on the amount of natural ability the dog is blessed with. Training can begin with basic obedience (sit, stay, down, come) and specific hunting skills. For example, dogs who hunt live birds are introduced to birds by three to six months of age, and start hunting or trialing at a year old. Training can also involve retrieving special bumpers and working on handling skills.

Hunt test

66. Dogsledding

Of all the organized sports activities, sledding probably requires the greatest lifestyle commitment. Fast, well-trained sled dog teams are the result of careful planning and hard work. Success in sledding depends on the *musher*'s (handler's) knowledge of kennel management, canine behavior, nutrition, veterinary care, dog psychology, physical conditioning, housing, and transportation.

Any dog of medium or larger size (35 pounds [15.9 kilograms] or more), can be considered a potential sled dog if she has a desire to pull and is *biddable* (obeys commands readily). In addition to the Siberian Husky, Samoyed, and Alaskan Malamute, many different breeds and mixed-breed dogs are successful sled dogs. Carefully selected mixed breeds can be found on many of the top competitive teams.

Dogsled races are divided into *sprint* races, *mid-distance* races, and *long-distance* races. Sprint races (4 to 25 miles [6.4 to 40 kilometers] per day) are usually two- or three-day events with heats run on successive days with the same dogs over the same course. Mid-distance races are either *heat races* of 14 to 80 miles (22.5 to 129 kilometers) per day, or *continuous races* of 100 to 200 miles (161 to 322 kilometers). These categories are informal and may overlap.

Long-distance races (200 to more than 1,000 miles [322 to 1,610 kilometers]) may be *continuous races* or *stage races*, in which participants run a different course each day, usually from a central staging location. The most famous long-distance race is the Iditarod Trail Sled Dog Race, held annually from Willow (near Anchorage) to Nome, Alaska, a distance of 1,161 miles (1,868 kilometers).

Both pure-bred and mixed-breed dogs are successful sled dogs.

Training

Training begins with early socialization so puppies become comfortable with people, as well as learning how to properly interact with other dogs. The harness is introduced at an early age. The puppy begins by pulling a small object—all done with lots of praise and positive reinforcement. At approximately six months of age, the puppy joins a small team of older dogs under the watchful eye of her owner, who ensures that her first experience running with a team is a positive one.

At a year old, training begins in earnest in the fall. The dog builds up her aerobic condition and muscle strength, and learns to run with the others as a team by pulling a cart on dirt or sand trails. The young dogs learn how to ignore distractions, respond to commands, and handle different trail conditions. Training begins with short, brief runs. The distance increases as the dogs build strength and stamina.

A dog that begins training as an adult needs to be introduced gradually to the harness, using praise and tasty treats. She must be comfortable wearing the harness before a light weight is added. Increase the weight gradually before attaching the sled. As in training a puppy, positive experiences, praise, and reinforcement are keys to the success of the training program for an adult dogsledder.

Another type of dogsled racing is the *freight race*, in which a specified weight per dog is carried in the sled. Races are also broken down by the maximum number of dogs allowed on each team, usually four, six, eight, or ten dogs, or unlimited (also called *open*).

Dog teams generally start one after another in equal time intervals, competing against the clock rather than directly against one another. *Mass starts*, where all of the dog teams start simultaneously, are popular in many parts of Canada.

Racing-sled dogs wear harnesses to which individual *tuglines* are snapped. The lines include short *neck lines* attached to each dog's collar to keep the dog in proper position. The dogs are hooked in pairs, with their tug lines attached to a central *gang line*.

Getting Started

The best way to enter the sport is to find a mentor in an experienced dog driver. The International Sled Dog Racing Association (ISDRA) provides contact information as well as a list of clubs to find mentorship opportunities. (See page 166.) Teams of at least four dogs can be made up of shared dogs from other members. In this way, prospective mushers and sled dogs can experience running with a team before making a total commitment to the lifestyle.

67. Skijoring

Skijoring provides an excellent winter workout for dogs and their owners. In skijoring, one to three dogs run in front of a handler who is on cross-country skis. The dogs wear pulling harnesses and are attached to the skier's belt by a 7- to 12-foot (2.1 to 3.7 meter) towline. When running with two or three dogs, the dogs are also connected to each other by necklines to keep them together. In skijor races, dogs provide extra power by pulling the handler along the trail.

Any dog who is energetic, is physically sound, and weighs more than 25 pounds (11.3 kilograms) can participate in skijor races.

Similar Sports

- Canicross—Running with a dog attached by a towline can be a great place to begin training and to get physically fit for skijoring.
- Snowboarding—Using a snowboard in place of cross-country skis is a variation of skijoring and is done recreationally.
- Grassjoring—Skiing on grass instead of snow can also be used for conditioning and training.

Dogs wear pulling harnesses and are attached by towlines to the skier's belt.

The top-ranked racing teams in the world are German short-haired pointers, pointer/Greyhound mixes, Alaskan Huskies, and crosses between these breeds. Dogs need to be well trained, be responsive to commands, and love to pull. Handlers must be confident on cross-country skis. Physical fitness is very important for both dogs and owners in this exciting sport.

Multiple dogs are connected to each other by necklines.

Training

Training begins by familiarizing the dog with the equipment: a pulling harness, towline, and belt. Allow the dog to wear the harness for short periods of time at first. When the dog is comfortable wearing the harness, attach a leash and let him walk ahead, encouraging him to pull. Add the towline and the skijor belt to familiarize the dog with all the equipment, training on foot before asking him to pull someone on skis. For safety reasons, practice unhooking the dog so it can be done quickly, and make sure his recall is reliable before going out onto a trail. Dogs must also be taught to respond to verbal commands for running forward, turning left and right, and stopping.

Getting Started

Three international organizations hold sanctioned skijor races. Often these races are done in conjunction with sled races. The International Sled Dog Racing Association (ISDRA) sanctions many races in the United States and Canada. The European Sled Dog Racing Association (ESDRA) provides sanctioned races in Europe. The International Federation of Sled Dog Sports (IFSDS) sanctions World Cup races all over the world, as well as a World Championship race every two years.

68. Canicross

The term *canicross* is of European origin, meaning to move cross-country with your dog.

Canicross is the sport of running or walking with the dog in a harness, pulling the owner along the course or trail. The owner's hands are free because the dog is attached at the belt, using equipment similar to that used in skijoring: a belt harness, a line with an integrated shock cord, and a harness for the dog.

Because canicross is a sport of endurance, both dog and handler need to train for slow-twitch muscle groups and cardio conditioning. A conditioning program for the dog and human to gradually gain strength and endurance is necessary.

Any size or breed of dog can participate in canicross. What matters most is that the dog possess a sound temperament, displaying good manners around other dogs and humans. Dogs come into close contact with other dogs and their owners at the start line or in passing one another during the race. Growling and baring of teeth is not tolerated.

Many people that start in this sport are already runners, but canicross can be done at a walk, and anyone at any fitness level

Training

In training a dog for canicross, owners must teach her to respond quickly to commands to stop, turn left or right, and heel to maneuver down hills. The dog is out in front of the owner, so it would be a great advantage to be able to use voice commands to signal her to turn, slow down, or stop.

can get started, train, and compete. Even children who are able to manage a dog can do canicross. Races are usually run on grass, dirt, or sand, all of which provide good cushioning for joint impact. Distances range from 3.1 to 6.2 miles (5 to 10 kilometers). Canicross is a great way for owners to get in good physical condition with their dog.

Getting Started

Although gaining in popularity in the United States, canicross is more frequently found in Europe, where it began. Dog Run Dog, a Vermont-based organization, sponsors canicross races throughout North America (see page 166).

Fun Activities to Do with Your Dog

There are many ways to get out, get fit, and bond with dogs. Many activities are great for any dog or owner, regardless of age or physical ability. The most important thing is to get up and get moving, get the dog motivated and stimulated, and enjoy the time spent with the dog. The following activities only require basic obedience. Dogs and owners can build up their fitness level while progressing in the activities at their own pace.

What Is Basic Obedience?

- Reliable Recall—The dog should come when *first* called, regardless of distractions (e.g., other dogs, other people, food, squirrels, and interesting odors).
- Sit or Down Stay—The dog should remain in the sit or down position until released by the owner.

69. Hiking

Hiking is a great fitness activity for owners and their dogs. Hiking outdoors in the fresh air provides both with a great stress-reducing, aerobic workout. Whether it is an hour's hike, a daylong hike, or a backpacking trip, hiking with a canine companion is a thoroughly enjoyable experience.

All dogs can participate; however, senior dogs and puppies should not be hiked for long distances. Short-muzzled dogs such as pugs or bulldogs should not be hiked vigorously or on steep trails, due to their lower oxygen intake. Dogs in good physical condition will enjoy hiking, but they must be conditioned for this activity. Start with short hikes and gradually build up to longer ones.

Hiking can be done in local parks, state parks, and some national parks. Check with local and state park authorities for information on trails that are dog friendly. Ask for specific information and restrictions concerning pets.

Some parks, for example, allow dogs without leashes, whereas others require them to always be leashed. Almost all will require hikers to clean up after their pet. Visit the agency's website to find out about the rules that apply to dogs *before* heading out to the park, and plan accordingly. Access information on national parks is available through the Internet (see page 166).

Always bring plenty of water for you and your dog. Dogs can become dehydrated, so carry water and a collapsible bowl with you at all times. Don't forget to bring along a leash and collar or harness. The dog should have his dog tags on his collar. If you do a lot of hiking,

consider inserting a microchip in your dog in case he gets lost. If camping overnight or for an all-day hike, bring dog food and treats to keep up his energy level, a blanket or dog jacket if the weather is questionable, a first-aid kit, and a favorite toy. The dog can carry his own food, water, jacket, and toy in a dog pack. Bring bags for cleaning up after the dog, or a shovel to bury pet waste, depending on the rules of the park. (Be responsible and dispose of both pet and human wastes outside the park, if the park's rules require that you do so.)

The dog should be well trained and under control, whether on or off-leash (follow any leash rules for that area), as a courtesy to other trail users and to protect local wildlife. Being under control will also protect him from dangers such as venomous snakes, skunks, porcupines, and such predators as bears and mountain lions. Be sure to find out about the local wildlife when you plan your hike. Also, find out where the nearest emergency veterinary clinic is to the hiking area and have a cell phone and an extra car key with you, so that you prevent becoming stranded.

Check the weather forecast for the area. Plan to hike in the morning or evening if daytime temperatures are high. Pack for cold weather with clothing layers; bring a jacket or blanket for the dog.

Observe the dog carefully for any physical distress. Allow him time to rest, seek shade, and stay hydrated. Take frequent rest and water breaks, preferably in the shade, no matter how well conditioned your dog is.

70. Beach Walk

Many dogs and humans enjoy a day at the beach. The sand beneath their paws and feet, the ocean water to swim in, and the brisk ocean breezes all add up to a relaxing, enjoyable experience. It's a great way to spend a day! Dogs that love to run and play and who love the water will enjoy going to the beach.

Where to Go

An increasing number of dog-friendly beaches throughout the United States and Canada allow dogs, both on and off-leash. DogFriendly.com has a list of more than two hundred dog-friendly beaches. Check for the beach near you, paying attention to the beach rules, and get going.

Beach walk

What to Bring

- Bring lots of fresh water and a bowl for the dog. Saltwater is not good for drinking. Excessive drinking of salt-water can cause diarrhea and vomiting.
- If you plan to spend the whole day at the beach, be sure to bring a beach umbrella to share with your dog.
- Bring toys that float and towels for drying the dog after he has been swimming.
- Bring bags for removing the dog's waste. The second most popular reason for banning dogs from beaches is dog waste left on the beach. Owners should *always* clean up after their pet out of respect for other beach-goers. Many town ordinances impose a fine on people who do not clean up after their pet.
- Bring a leash and a collar. Some beaches welcome dogs but do not allow off-leash play. The most popular reason for banning dogs from beaches is disregard for leash laws. Many beaches have banned dogs because of concern over incidents between dogs or between dogs and people. Dog owners need to be courteous to other beach-goers and follow leash laws to preserve their access to and enjoyment of the beach.

71. Canoeing and Kayaking with Dogs

Canoeing and kayaking are becoming increasingly popular activities. Canoeing with a canine companion is a great way to explore the waterways. Dogs have a way of making the activities we share with them more fun.

Any dog can enjoy being in a canoe or kayak. Dogs that enjoy swimming and playing in the water really take to these activities, but it is not necessary for them to do so to have some fun. Dogs that do not like getting wet but want to be with their owner find riding in the boat enjoyable. Dogs that love to swim are happy swimming alongside the canoe or kayak.

Before jumping into a canoe with your dog (tempting, as it looks so easy to do), it is a good idea to get some professional instruction and advice. When renting or purchasing a canoe or kayak, look for stable canoes or kayaks well suited to paddling with a dog along inside.

Items to pack include a waterproof bag for dog food, a folding bowl for water, towels, a leash that floats, pet waste bags, a portable camping shovel, and a first-aid kit (make sure it contains tape, bandages, and a dog thermometer). Bring lots of bottled water for the dog and paddler.

Dog owners should treat their dog droppings according to the prevailing rules for human waste on the waterway along which they are boating. If the waterway is in a pack-it-out zone, bag the pet waste and throw it out at the end of the trip into an appropriate container. Otherwise, bring along a small camp shovel to bury it.

Paddle sports offer lots of opportunities to explore nature's waterways, experience the serenity of the outdoors, and enjoy the company of our dogs.

Training

First, assess the dog: does he love the water? Does the dog know how to swim? Teaching the dog to get into the canoe or kayak should first be done on dry land so he gets used to being in the boat. Once the dog is comfortable, float the canoe in shallow water so he can get the feel of the boat floating. When the dog is ready for longer boat trips, you may want to consider a canine lifejacket for your dog before starting out, in case he tires from swimming or is hurt.

Kayaking

72. Mountain Biking

Mountain biking with a dog can provide great exercise and companionship for both the owner and the dog. There are many great trails to ride and parks to explore on a mountain bike; taking a dog along can make it a much more interesting experience. Dogs are attuned to nature on so many levels—sight, sound, and especially scent—that watching dogs frolic, chase, and explore the great outdoors can be a joyful experience.

Training

Like people, dogs need to become fit to enjoy mountain biking. Begin slowly with the dog, by biking short distances several times per week, working up to longer bike rides. Start with short loops instead of long out-and-back trips. Be sure to bike on dirt or grass paths, avoiding concrete and asphalt, as this is hard on the dog's joints and the pads of her feet. The health and safety of the dog is the most important consideration when mountain biking. When riding with a dog, always be alert for natural and man-made hazards as well as attentive to her general condition.

The dog's age will also limit the distance and pace (speed) of the ride. An older dog may not be able to go for long distances, and may need a slower pace than a younger dog. Puppies should *not* begin biking or any endurance training until after they reach six months of age. At six months of age, they should only be taken on short rides with soft footing. A dog's growth plates are not closed until they reach eighteen months of age, so until then, they should not be taken on long bike rides. Strenuous exercise can cause joint problems and the early onset of arthritis, so it is important not to stress the limbs of young dogs by overexercising. Do not increase the bike's speed down hills, as this puts a lot of stress on the dog's knee and elbow joints. Don't go downhill any faster than the dog can trot.

Overheating is a major concern with dogs. Avoid riding in the middle of the day —ride either early in the morning or late in the afternoon. Keep your dog hydrated, even in cool weather. Be sure to bring along water and a collapsible bowl for her to drink at regular and frequent intervals. Cooling the dog down at the end of the ride by hosing her legs, chest, and abdomen will speed her recovery.

As a general rule, do not bike any breed of dog an hour before or after a meal. Bloat can be fatal. Some breeds are more prone to bloat than others. For more information on symptoms and a list of breeds that are at high risk, consult your veterinarian or the Internet.

Almost any breed of dog can enjoy mountain biking with their owners. However, this activity is not recommended for short-muzzled breeds, because it requires a large oxygen intake and traveling over long distances. Breeds such as pugs and bulldogs have difficulty with oxygen intake, due to their short muzzles. Medium-size breeds with moderate coats are best at this activity, but even small and large dogs can enjoy it as long as the cyclist takes their size and fitness into consideration.

Check with the local or state park services for dog-friendly mountain bike trails. Some parks do not allow dogs due to wildlife or other concerns. Be a responsible dog owner. Bag dog waste to dispose of outside the area, and control the dog around other track users, especially horseback riders.

Mountain biking

73. Cross-Country Skiing

Cross-country skiing with dogs is a wonderful way to enjoy winter sport activities with a canine partner. Unlike skijoring, cross-country skiing with dogs is generally an off-leash activity. When leashes are needed, the dog moves alongside and does not pull the skier. It is enjoyed purely as a recreational activity.

Any breed of dog can go with his owner on a cross-country skiing trip. Caution should be taken with older dogs and short-muzzled breeds such as pugs or bulldogs. Smaller dogs may have trouble working their way through snow. Medium-size to large breeds will have an easier time at this activity. Puppies love to play in snow, but they should not be expected, nor is it advisable, for them to keep up with a cross-country skier.

Make sure the dog is physically fit before taking him on a cross-country ski adventure.

Running through snow is very strenuous for dogs and humans. Although temperatures are cool, a dog can become overheated; hydration is very important. Be sure to bring fresh water and a collapsible bowl for the dog, and make frequent rest stops. Always be aware of the dog's physical condition.

Keep the dog close to you and do not let him visit other skiers or dogs. This will keep the dog safe and prevent other skiers from being knocked over. Keep the dog leashed wherever leash laws are in effect. Dogs must usually be on leash until they get to the trail head, and need to be well behaved on off-leash trails as well as within sight at all times. In some ski areas, chasing wildlife is prohibited. Do not let the dog chase after wild animals, and always bag and dispose of your dog's waste outside the recreational area.

Cross-country skiing

74. Nordic Walking

Nordic walking is a great way to get fit and can help get a dog in shape as well. Nordic walking is low-impact fitness walking that uses special lightweight poles. The poles provide support to the human's lower body, relieving stress on the ankles, hips, and knees during walking. Nordic walking also burns more calories than just walking for the same distance at the same speed.

Give the dog adequate time to relieve herself before starting out, so she can walk without distraction. Once the walk begins, the dog should move alongside at a good working pace and not be allowed to sniff or lag behind. Use a hands-free lead that attaches to the waist, to prevent the leash from getting entangled in the poles. If the dog likes to pull, use a harness or head leader that discourages pulling, to prevent her from pulling you off balance.

Be sure to take fresh water and a collapsible bowl. A water bottle can be tucked into a fanny pack, or the dog can wear a backpack and carry her own water.

Nordic walking is easy on the joints and gives both dog and owner an excellent aerobic workout.

75. Horseback Trail Riding

Riding a horse provides a good physical workout and a chance to enjoy the great outdoors. From cow dogs to coach dogs, dogs have a long history of interacting with horses and people. Dogs take part in activities such as fox hunting, herding, road trials, and trail rides, all of which bring them into contact with horses.

Almost any dog can learn to safely accompany horses, and most horses can become accustomed to the presence of dogs. The dog should be physically sound and fit, display a calm and quiet demeanor around livestock, and be able to respond to verbal commands from its owner on horseback.

The horse should be calm and be used to the presence of dogs. Do not trail ride with a dog if the horse kicks at dogs or other horses. Make sure the horse is experienced with trail riding and dogs before attempting a ride.

Dogs should be well trained with basic obedience commands—sit, (lie) down, stay, and come. The owner must be able to control the dog from horseback. This control is necessary when encountering other riders or hikers on the trail, as well as crossing roads, going through gates, and following the horse.

Your dog should be fit to enjoy trail riding. Begin slowly, by taking the dog on short rides and building up to longer ones. Do not go too fast—he should not have to sustain a pace faster than a trot to keep up with the horse.

The dog's age will limit its ride distance. Older dogs may not be able to go long distances, and require a slower pace. Dogs at six months of age should only be taken on short rides with soft footing. Growth plates are not closed until after eighteen months of age; until then, they should not be over-exercised. Strenuous exercise can cause joint problems and arthritis later in life.

Overheating is a major concern with dogs. Do not take a dog out riding in the heat of the day—ride in the early morning or later afternoon when it is cooler. Keep your dog hydrated even in cool weather. Be sure to bring along water and a collapsible bowl for him to drink at regular and frequent intervals.

Training

Introduce the dog and horse by taking the dog to the barn on a leash and keeping him around while doing cleanup chores and feeding. Hiking the dog while leading the horse is another safe way to introduce the horse and the dog to each other.

Keeping track of the dog while on horseback can be a challenge, especially if you are riding in high grass or if the dog likes to explore on his own. Attach a loud bell to the dog's collar, so that he can be heard from a distance. Call the dog back regularly and reward with a treat to encourage him to return when called.

Before going on a trail ride, check with local forest and park services for rules and safety governing trail rides. Be familiar with local wildlife and other potential hazards. Most important, go out and enjoy the great outdoors with man's best friends, the dog and the horse.

76. Going to a Dog Park

Taking a dog to the dog park can be a fun adventure. Dogs love to socialize with other dogs, while their owners can get together with other dog lovers. Dog parks are excellent places to work on basic obedience training (*focused attention* in particular), and the dog can be rewarded for her attention with off-leash play after working.

Finding the Best Dog Park

There are several things to look for when choosing a dog park:

- Fenced dog parks are safer—fences keep the dogs out of traffic.
- Look for a double-fenced, double-gated, or graduated entrance to the park that allows the dogs to come through without letting other dogs out of the park.
- The dog park should have shade and lots of sources for water throughout for both dogs and owners.
- Ample trash cans and waste cleanup stations should be spread throughout the park to encourage owners to clean up after the dogs.
- If the owner intends to exercise while the dog is playing or the dog needs to be walked for exercise, look for a dog park that has a path or walkway running through it.

Safety First

Keep these important safety points in mind when using a dog park:

- Dogs must be fully vaccinated before going to the dog park. Puppies or adult dogs that have not been vaccinated can be exposed to germs and diseases such as kennel cough or parvo virus. Puppies under four months of age should absolutely not go to the dog park until they have had all three series of recommended vaccinations.

You can make all kinds of new friends at the dog park.

- Never leave your dog unattended at the dog park. Although it is easy to get distracted at the park, the purpose of going to the dog park is to be with and interact with your dog. Walking, playing, and being attentive to your dog makes the visits to the dog park a positive experience.

- Do not bring a female dog that is in season to the dog park. Not only is there a risk of the female's being bred, but also females in season can cause other male dogs to fight with one another.

- Let your dog off the leash as soon as you arrive. Leashed dogs may feel threatened and growl or bark when off-leash dogs greet them. Keep walking when you enter the dog park. This keeps the off-leash area neutral territory.

- Always observe all of the rules posted at your local dog park. Each town has its own set of rules and regulations.

Dog park

77. Surfing

Dog surfing is becoming very popular wherever there are beaches with surf. Surf dogs can ride the waves alone on their board or with their owners. Competitions for dog surfing are cropping up along the southern coast of California. Surfing dogs can be found anywhere there are surfers, dogs, good waves, and great beaches—Hawaii, New Zealand, Australia, South Africa, and Southeast Asia. This is an up-and-coming sport for dogs and their surfer owners.

Any breed or mixed breed of dog can surf. Dogs who like water and enjoy swimming take to it very quickly. Dogs compete against dogs of similar size at surfing events. Free dog surfing lessons are usually available to entered dogs.

In surfing competitions, the dogs are judged on a variety of skills, including the

Training

The dog's surfboard should be a foam board, approximately 7 to 8 feet (2.1 to 2.4 meters) long. Begin by rewarding the dog for getting on the board on dry land. Reward her for standing, sitting, and lying down on the board. Tip the board from side to side and wiggle it while the dog balances on the board; reward with treats. When she is comfortable on the board, place the board in still water and lure her to climb on. Push the board around in the water, slowly at first and then with more movement as the dog gets used to it. Once she is completely comfortable, the board can be taken into an area with small waves. Let the dog ride small waves until she becomes very confident on the surfboard. Consider a canine life vest to make every ride a good time.

Surfing

length of the ride, the size of the wave, and each dog's confidence on the board. There are also competitions for dog and human surfing teams, where both the dog and owner are on the board together.

Several groups, especially in California, offer surfing lessons for dogs and sponsor surfing events. There are also instruction books on dog surfing (see page 166).

78. Skateboarding

Dogs on skateboards are not an uncommon sight. Many dogs like to chase skateboards, as well as climb on and enjoy the ride. Skateboarding is a great fitness activity for dogs and their owners to enjoy outdoors. Some owners walk alongside their dog, others skateboard along with their dog, and still others ride on the board with their dog.

Any dog can learn to skateboard. Small to medium-size dogs are more commonly found skateboarding because they fit more comfortably on the board. The best skateboarding dogs are bulldogs and Jack Russell Terriers. These dogs are tenacious and love to chase as well as ride skateboards. Very small dogs can ride on the board with their owner.

Be sure to have your dog skateboard in a safe environment. Sidewalks along busy streets could be dangerous where the skateboard can roll off the sidewalk and into the street. Parks, fenced yards, or skate parks that allow dogs are the best choices. Some city parks also offer skateboarding areas.

Training

Begin by placing the skateboard on a carpeted or a grassy surface so it does not roll easily. Reward the dog for getting up on the board and balancing on the board. When the dog is comfortable on the board, place the skateboard on a smoother surface and roll him slowly along on the skateboard. Steady the board in the beginning when the dog hops on. Gradually allow the board to roll when he hops on it. The force of the dog's hopping on and off the board will roll the board along. Many dogs who enjoy skateboarding will figure out how to use their feet to propel the board forward.

Skateboarding

79. Dog-a-thons

Dog-a-thons are distance walk/run events that allow dogs to accompany their owners. Dog-a-thons are usually races whose proceeds go to a charity, such as the local animal shelter. Many organizations worldwide regularly sponsor dog-a-thons, and the proceeds are used toward such issues as homeless pets. Exercising with your dog to help a good cause is rewarding both physically and emotionally.

Any dog can participate in a dog-a-thon. Dogs need to be as fit as their owners, who will be participating with them in the race. Dog-a-thons are usually 3 or 6 miles (5 or 10 kilometers) long.

A canine participant should have some basic obedience training and be well socialized. When walking or jogging within a large crowd, it is important that she be a *good citizen*. Dogs aggressive toward people or other dogs should not participate in dog-a-thons.

Training

When training for the dog-a-thon, begin walking a reasonable distance at a comfortable pace for the dog. Gradually increase the distance of the walk, but keep the pace comfortable for her. Puppies and older dogs should not participate in activities that require walking for long distances or strenuous exercise for a long period of time.

Be sure to bring water and a collapsible bowl for the dog, to keep her hydrated on practice walks and during the dog-a-thon.

Playing Games with Your Dog

Playing with your dog fulfills two very important needs for him. It provides a bonding experience that is more than just being with you. It inherently shows who the leader is—who starts and ends the game and provides the attention and approval he seeks from his leader. Second, it gives him a fun, physical outlet for his energy. Many problem behaviors in dogs can be resolved with regular game playing. It gives the dog a great way to get rid of mental and emotional stresses that build up over the course of a day. A tired dog is a happy dog.

The same advantages can apply to dog owners. Establishing and reinforcing your role as the dog's leader can help build your self-confidence and positively affect other areas of your life. The negative effects of stress on your physical well-being can be reduced by physical activity. Playing with your dog is a win-win situation.

Games can be used to reinforce important obedience behaviors (Recall Back 'n' Forth for a reliable recall or Stay Sprints for a solid stay) in a fun, positive, nonstressful way. They can also be used to build physical endurance (Fetch and Swim), acceleration (Two-Toy Fetch) and strength (Tug-of-War). Remember always to be aware of the dog's physical condition and quit the game before he becomes fatigued. Have water readily available.

Training Tip

Playing games with your dog is an important training tool. It builds value into toys and playing with her owner (increases *toy drive*). When training a dog for competition, it gives the owner or handler a very effective tool to use as reinforcement to train the behavior needed for the activity. It is especially effective in increasing speed and focusing attention.

80. Fetch

Fetch is a fantastic game to play with dogs. Most dogs really enjoy retrieving thrown items. Playing with toys and working on retrieving when dogs are puppies is the easiest way to train the fetch.

Begin with the dog or puppy on a leash. Get him excited about a toy by dragging it along the ground in front of him until he mouths the toy. Pull the toy gently but quickly away and toss it low along the ground, just a couple of feet (half a meter) away. Let the dog run to pick it up. Once the dog has picked up the toy, reel him in on the leash with the toy and tug with the dog. Repeat the exercise. Once the dog is excited about retrieving the toy from 2 feet (0.6 meter) away, increase the distance a little. Increase the length of the leash until the dog can retrieve the toy using the full length of a flexi lead or long line.

Keep the leash on the dog until he no longer needs to be reeled in with the toy. Once the dog is repeatedly returning with the toy without any assistance from the leash, he can be allowed off the leash for the retrieve game.

Go Fetch

1. With the dog on a leash, attract his attention to the toy.

2. Quickly toss the toy a few feet (half a meter) away.

3. Let the dog run to the toy and pick it up.

4. Reel the dog back with the leash and tug the toy with him, for the reward. Increase the distance of the throw until the dog is retrieving the toy on a flexi lead or long line.

step 1

step 2

step 3

step 4

81. Fetch and Swim

Swimming is a great endurance activity for dogs because of the low impact on their joints. Adding the fetch will keep them excited about the exercise. If swimming in a pool, it is best for the dog to remain in the water so she does not get out of the pool and run around and slip. Stand on the steps of the pool, where the dog will try to exit the pool. Take the toy from the dog while she is still in the water and toss the toy back into the water. She will swim back and forth for the toy without leaving the water. Exiting the water to return the toy is safe if the dog is at the beach or a lake. Always be aware of water temperatures, to avoid hypothermia. Do not swim the dog to the point of exhaustion, because drowning is a danger when a dog becomes tired.

Consider a canine life jacket for longer swims and for dogs swimming in unfamiliar waters.

82. Two-Toy Fetch

Use two toys of equal value when playing this game. Hold the first toy in one hand, and hold the dog by the collar with your other hand. Have the second toy tucked in the waistband of your trousers.

Toss the first toy 10 feet (3 m) away, releasing the dog's collar and encouraging her to get the toy. As the dog runs to the first toy, drop the second toy to the ground behind you and run to the dog for a game of tug with the first toy.

Take the dog by the collar and take the first toy away from her. Hide the first toy behind your back and send the dog back to the second toy that is on the ground. As the dog goes to the second toy, drop the first toy on the ground behind you, and run over to the dog for a game of tug.

Repeat these steps a few times, but always stop playing while the dog still wants to play. That will make the dog even more eager to play the next time.

1. With the second toy tucked in the waistband of your trousers, toss the first toy ten feet (3 m) away, releasing the dog's collar and encouraging her to get the toy.

2. As the dog runs to the first toy, drop the second toy to the ground behind you, and run to the dog for a game of tug with the first toy.

3. Hide the first toy behind your back and send the dog back to the second toy that is on the ground. As the dog goes to the second toy, drop the first toy on the ground behind you.

4. Run over to the dog for a game of tug.

5. Send the dog back to the second toy, and drop the first toy behind your back.

6. Run over to the dog for a game of tug. Repeat the game several times, but always stop the game before the dog tires out.

step 1

step 2

step 3

step 4

step 5

step 6

83. Fish for a Dog

This is a great game for puppies and adult dogs. It is especially fun for dogs that like to chase toys but are not good at bringing them back. Several companies manufacture a toy on a long stick and string, but it is easy to make one with a pole and rope, or a lunge whip for horses. Simply secure a fun toy to the end of the line or whip, and drag the toy around on the ground in front of the dog until he is chasing the toy and grabs it in his mouth. Be sure to let the dog get the toy and tug it quite often, so that he does not give up the chase game.

1. Drag a toy in a line along the ground to engage the puppy to chase it.
2. Allow the puppy to catch and tug at the toy.

step 1

step 2

84. Tug-of-War

Most puppies will tug easily. If your puppy does not readily tug the toy, begin by dragging the toy along the ground until she takes hold of the toy. Tug a little and let the puppy win the toy. Do not yank the toy out of the puppy's mouth because this will discourage tugging. Tug only as hard as she tugs and build her confidence by allowing her to win the toy. At the end of the game, however, the human must win the toy and end the game. To build more confidence, pry the toy away from the puppy to win, instead of demanding that she drop the toy.

step 1

1. Drag the toy along the ground to encourage the puppy to chase and pounce on the toy.
2. The puppy takes hold of the toy.
3. Tug with the puppy with the same amount of force that she is tugging with you.

step 2

step 3

85. Nose Games

Teaching dogs specific nose games can be fun and challenging. Dogs use their nose naturally, but they must be taught to use their nose when directed by their owner. This game teaches a dog to follow a trail to an article of clothing or a toy by rewarding him along the way with treats.

Place a harness and a leash or long line on the dog. Leave him in a down stay or in a crate. Take a toy with you. Pick a starting point and walk a path, dropping lots of treats along the path where you step. At the end of the path, place the toy or article down and put treats on or in it. Go back to the dog using the same path as the treats. Using the leash, take the dog to the beginning of the path. Point down to the treats and ask the dog to look for the toy ("Find it"). The dog follows the path and gets lots of treats along the way, with a jackpot at the end. As the dog plays the game more often, gradually use fewer treats on the path but leave a big treat jackpot on the toy. The dog will learn to follow the scent of the path to get the treat reward. This game is used to begin training scent work (tracking). It can be played outdoors or in the house. Working this game on different surfaces will make the dog better at scent work.

step 1

1. Place an article with a treat jackpot at the end of the treat trail.

2. Indicate the trail by pointing at the beginning of the trail and telling the dog to look for it ("Find it").

3. The dog follows the trail and eats the treats along the way.

4. The dog finds the article and gets the jackpot.

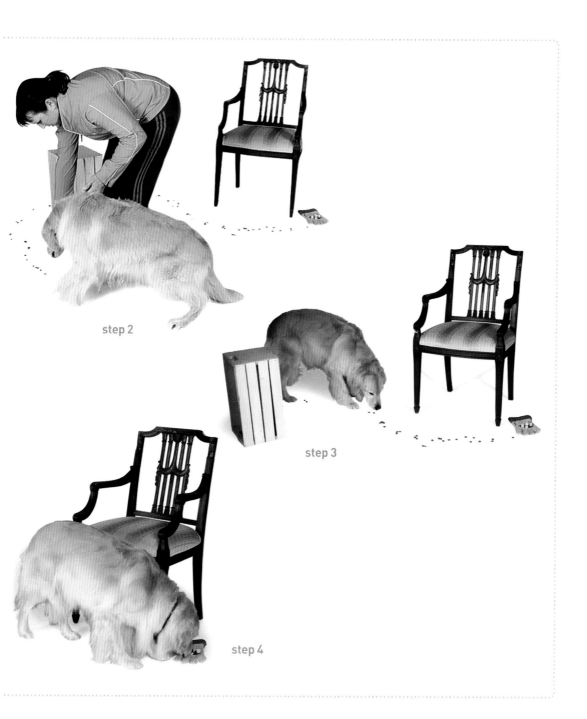

step 2

step 3

step 4

86. Recall Back 'n' Forth

This game requires two people the dog knows well and likes. Have each person hold delicious treats or the dog's favorite toys to make them more attractive targets. The people should stand approximately 50 feet (15 meters) or more apart, with the first person holding the dog by the collar or placing his or her arms around the dog's chest. Have the second person call for the dog excitedly, using her name and the recall word ("Come"). When the dog starts pulling to go to the second person, release the dog and let her run to that person. When she reaches the second person, she should be rewarded with treats or play with the toy. The second person now holds the dog and the first person calls excitedly for the dog to come. When the dog pulls to go to the first person, release the dog and let her run back to the first person, who rewards her with treats and toys. This is an excellent game for improving the dog's recall.

1. One person restrains the dog while the second person runs away, calling the dog excitedly.
2. When the dog pulls to go to the person calling her, she is released to run to that person.
3. The second person now restrains the dog while the other person calls the dog excitedly.
4. When the dog pulls to go to the person calling, she is released.

step 1

step 2

step 3

step 4

87. Stay Sprints

A prerequisite for this game is that the dog must know and obey a stay command. A big plus to this exercise is that it takes only one person to play the game with one or more dogs. Place the dog in a stay (sit, down, or stand). Jog away from the dog for at least 50 feet (15 meters). Call and release the dog to run to you, as you run away from him. When the dog catches you, reward him with a treat or a thrown toy. This is an excellent training game to reinforce the stay command, improve the dog's recall, and teach him to run quickly when released.

step 1

1. Leave the dog in a stay position and jog away.
2. Call the dog excitedly from about 50 feet (15 meters) away, releasing him to run to you.
3. When the dog catches up to you, reward with a treat, tug, or thrown toy.

step 2

Get That Dog, or Keep Away

Some dogs like to play keep away with their toys. Once the dog knows a command for bringing a toy to you, teach her a command for the keep away game. Chase the dog for the toy around the room or yard. When both dog and owner are tired, give the dog the command to bring and relinquish the toy and thus conclude the game. The owner should always end the game by obtaining the toy.

step 3

Puppy Activities

Having a puppy is one of the great joys in life. Puppies make you smile and laugh. They have seemingly bound-less energy and no boundaries. Every activity provides a training opportunity for a puppy. They are great sponges, absorbing the lessons of everyday life. Just keeping up with their antics can provide lots of physical exercise for the owner!

Many of the following activities focus on ensuring the safety and physical well-being of the dog the puppy will grow into. Going for a walk may seem like a mundane activity, but it is important in setting up her relationship with her owner outside of the home, and in beginning a routine of daily physical exercise.

The Hold-the-Collar game gets the puppy used to someone reaching for her collar without running away, whereas restrained recalls teach the puppy to run quickly back to her owner when called. Some puppies need to learn to enjoy getting wet (Pool Play), especially if they are working dogs, because getting wet is the fastest way to cool off an overheated dog.

Get This Toy reinforces the owner's role as the leader—the toy the owner has is always the best toy to play with. Race Mama to the Toy is a confidence builder (the puppy gets to win the race), which builds drive for competitive games. Nose Touches also become useful in positioning the dog for an activity.

Remember to use lots of praise, treats, and toys when training puppies for any activity. Always keep in mind that puppies respond best to positive reinforcement, not negative corrections, so set up the training steps to ensure their success and reward. Keep sessions short and lengthen them as the puppy grows older. End the activity before the puppy quits.

Early Socialization

Puppies are taught how to behave with other dogs by their mother, up to the time they leave for their new home at about eight weeks old. After that, it is up to their owners to provide opportunities to interact with other dogs appropriately. Be aware of other dogs' reactions as well as a puppy's actions when meeting unfamiliar dogs.

It is just as important to socialize the puppy with other people, especially children. Very small children move differently and do not know how to approach puppies and dogs. After the puppy has been fully immunized, take him to different places and introduce him to different people. These early experiences will help the puppy grow into a dog that is able to deal calmly with new situations and people.

88. Going for a Walk

Walking puppies and dogs is an important way to establish leadership, promotes owner-dog bonding, and is great exercise for the owner and the dog. Walking the dog for at least 30 minutes every day is recommended by most dog trainers.

Before starting the walk, allow the puppy to relieve himself. Once the walk begins, do not allow the puppy to sniff or potty. The walk is for exercise, not exploring. Walk vigorously and deliberately, leading him on the walk. At the end of the walk, allow the puppy time to relieve himself again before going back into the house or yard.

It is important to know that it is not safe to walk puppies under the age of four months in public areas. They have not completed the recommended series of vaccinations and are at risk of contracting diseases such as parvo virus and distemper. Once the full series of vaccinations has been administered, the puppy can walk safely in parks or on public sidewalks.

Going for a walk

89. Hold-the-Collar Game

Many puppies and dogs do not like to be led by the collar. There are times when it would be helpful to be able to take hold of the collar to guide the dog gently into the car or into a crate, or simply to put the leash on. Teaching the puppy or dog to enjoy being held or led by the collar is an important tool that can be taught in a fun way.

Start out with treats and a clicker. Touch the puppy's collar, click when your hand touches the collar, and give the puppy a treat. Repeat this exercise over and over again, gradually taking hold of the collar a little longer each time, until you can pull on the collar and the puppy takes a step toward you. Reward each touch, hold, or pull. Lots of fast, fun repetitions will make the puppy enjoy being led by the collar.

step 1

step 2

1. With puppy sitting in front of you, touch her collar and click the clicker.

2. Give the puppy a treat.

3. Hold the puppy's collar with one hand, and hold a treat in front of her in your other hand. Reward her and click the clicker when she holds the position.

4. Gently pull on the puppy's collar and click/reward her as she comes forward to get the treat.

step 3

step 4

90. Get This Toy

Set many toys of equal value out on the ground at your feet. Pick up a toy and engage the puppy to play with only that toy. Let go of the toy and grab another toy. Play with it along the ground until the puppy lets go of the other toy and takes hold of the one you have. Play with the puppy, then let go and grab another toy, and so on. Continue with this game until no matter what you pick up, the puppy drops what he has and goes for the toy you have. The toy you pick is always the best toy to play with.

step 1

step 5

1. Kneel with the puppy, with an assortment of toys in front.
2. Engage the puppy with one of the toys.
3. Let go of the toy the puppy is tugging and reach for another toy.
4. Engage the puppy with the new toy.
5. Let go of the toy the puppy is tugging and reach for another toy.

step 2

step 3

step 4

91. Race Mama (or Papa) to the Toy

Hold the puppy by the collar and throw a favorite toy 6 to 10 feet (1.8 to 3 meters) away. Give the puppy a little push back as you let go of his collar and try to race him to the toy. Reach for the toy, but let the puppy get to the toy and pick it up. This will promote drive in the puppy and gets him motivated to run fast to retrieve. It is also a great workout for the owner.

step 1

1. Drag the toy on the ground to entice the puppy to play.
2. Throw the toy while holding the puppy by the collar.
3. Give a little tug backward on the collar, let go, and race the puppy toward the toy.
4. Reach for the toy, but let the puppy get the toy and pick it up, allowing him to win the race.

step 2

step 4

step 3

92. Restrained Recalls

Have a helper hold the puppy by the collar or around her chest. Have a toy or treat pouch with you to entice the puppy to want to come to you. Run away from the puppy, calling her enthusiastically. When the puppy strains against the collar to get to you, the helper releases the puppy and lets her run to you. When the puppy catches up to you, reward her by playing with a toy or giving her a tasty treat for coming quickly when called. This is a great, fun way to exercise for the human and the dog.

step 1

step 2

step 3

1. A helper holds the puppy while the owner holds toys or a food pouch.
2. A helper holds the puppy while the owner runs away, excitedly calling to the puppy.
3. A helper releases the puppy when she pulls to go to the owner.
4. The puppy is rewarded with a game of tug or treats, when she catches up with the owner.

step 4

93. Pool Play

Playing in a kiddie pool can be great fun. If the puppy enjoys toys, throwing floating toys into a shallow kiddie pool is a great way to get him to like getting in the water and swimming. Getting your puppy to enjoy water will become important later in life when he is working hard and needs to cool off in warm temperatures. First play with the puppy so that he is warm and panting a little. He will then enjoy getting into the cool water. If the puppy does not play with toys, use a clicker and tasty treats to lure him one foot at a time into the shallow water. Click and reward each time he puts his feet into the water. Soon the puppy will be offering to jump into the water for a treat. As he becomes more confident with stepping into the pool, add water to make it deeper. Just putting his feet in the water is helpful because dogs cool themselves off through the pads of their feet.

Dog in kiddie pool

94. Teaching the Balance Cushion

Introducing puppies to a Pilates balance cushion helps build confidence, balance, and dexterity. It will also help develop skills used later for strengthening and stretching exercises. Use small, delicious treats to reward the puppy for stepping onto the balance cushion. Use a clicker to mark the behavior of stepping onto the cushion and balancing on it. The clicker will help the puppy learn the behavior faster. Refer to the sections on stretching and strengthening (pages 34 to 43) to learn fun games you can play with the balance cushion.

step 1

1. Place the balance cushion on the ground in front of the puppy, and face him.
2. Use a treat to lure the puppy to step onto the balance cushion.
3. The puppy steps onto the balance cushion and balances without the treat lure.
4. Reward with a treat.

step 2

step 4

step 3

95. Nose Touches

This is a fun interactive trick for dogs that gets them coming to your side by touching their nose to either hand. This game is easy to teach puppies. Begin by enclosing a tasty treat in one hand. When the dog's nose touches the hand, give the treat. A clicker can be used to mark the behavior of the nose touching the hand. This will help the puppy learn to do the behavior faster, and move on to a touch without the food lure. Reward every time the nose touches whichever hand is offered. Using a clicker to pinpoint the nose touch can speed this training process. The hand can be moved to different positions so that the puppy follows that hand to touch it. Some trainers like to see the puppy jump up a bit to hit the hand with her nose. It is a fun game for puppies and can be useful in controlling the position of the dog.

step 1

1. Hold a treat in one hand, palm facing outward.
2. When the puppy touches the palm of the hand with her nose, let her take the treat.
3. Offer the open palm hand again without the treat in it.
4. The puppy touches the palm of the hand with her nose, looking for the treat.
5. Reward with a treat from the other hand.

step 2

step 3

step 4

step 5

Finding More Puppy Friends

Being around other dogs is important for puppy socialization. Find neighbors or friends who walk their friendly dogs and meet them during the week for regular walks to help with your puppy's socialization skills. It will also provide a good opportunity to exercise the puppy as well as her owner. Another fun play group idea would be to meet friends or neighbors with friendly dogs at a local dog park for some play time and socialization.

Senior Dog Activities

This progression cannot be stopped, but it does not need to significantly diminish the dog's quality of life. It becomes more important to set aside 20 to 30 minutes every day to spend time with the senior dog. Take a slow walk around the block or a quick swim in the pool, do a couple of strengthening exercises with lots of praise and treats, or practice rally moves or tracking exercises. Do something different every day, and you can expect your senior dog to stay alert and active.

Senior dogs need strengthening exercises to keep them flexible and healthy. They need activity for their mind and body to stay sharp and active. Low-impact activities are best for the senior dog.

Just like their owners, dogs age at different rates, with the larger breeds reaching their senior years earlier than small dogs. They also have a shorter life expectancy. A Great Dane can start showing signs of old age at the age of seven and have a life expectancy of nine to eleven years, whereas a mini poodle can still be happily doing agility at seven and expect to live another ten years. Both can experience hearing loss (usually occurs first), reduced vision, and weakening of the muscles during the last few years of life.

A Word about Nutrition for Senior Dogs

As dogs age, their ability to digest poor-quality food and to compensate for too much or too little of particular nutrients diminishes. They may have trouble with changes in diet and with digesting and chewing bones. Look over the list of ingredients on the dog's food label and make sure he is getting top-quality sources of protein and vitamins.

The senior dog's decrease in physical activity should be accompanied by a similar decrease in calories consumed. Obesity in animals is associated with cardiovascular problems, diabetes, arthritis, cancer, and a shorter life span. Much of the senior dog's physical fitness is determined by his weight.

Strengthening Exercises

Exercises that strengthen the hindquarters and lower back are important for dogs throughout their life. These exercises pay a big dividend once the dog passes into his senior years, when muscle weakness and arthritis can make it difficult to walk, climb stairs, and potty. Start slowly if the dog is not used to these exercises—don't ask for more than a couple of repetitions at first, and increase the amount of time you ask him to hold the position by only a couple of seconds at a time. Keep sessions short, perhaps asking for a sit-up or stand-down-stand for his morning treat. Vary the routine by asking for different exercises on different days and skipping a day every few days. Keep it fun and interesting to keep his mind alert and sharp.

96. Sit Up and Beg

One of the best exercises for senior dogs is to sit up and beg. Sitting up strengthens their hindquarter, back, and abdominal muscles. Often in senior dogs, hindquarter muscles tend to atrophy from diminishing use. Sitting-up exercises will help keep the back end strong, to ensure that senior dogs can get up and down easily on their own.

97. Stand-Down-Stand

Stand-down-stand is another excellent exercise for senior dogs because it strengthens all four legs and their abdominal muscles. The stand-down-stand exercise will keep senior dogs flexible and able to get up and down on their own.

98. Tugging

Tugging a toy provides a good strengthening exercise for senior dogs. Most dogs love to tug and play with their owner and other dogs. Tugging works the back-end and neck muscles.

Tug low so the dog does not lift off the ground to tug.

99. Endurance Exercises

Exercises and activities that have a low impact on the dog's body are best for the senior dog. A senior dog needs to get moving and keep moving to retain muscle tone and sensory awareness. Let the dog set the pace and enjoy the time set aside for each activity. Don't forget a nice session of stretching after walking or swimming. A dog thoroughly enjoys a good stretch and gentle massage by her owner. It is also a good chance for the owner to feel for lumps and injuries (e.g., sore spots), which are borne without complaint by dogs.

Swimming is the best endurance exercise for the senior dog. Swimming is low impact and excellent for strengthening the cardiovascular system, as well as working all the muscles in the body. Never leave a senior dog unattended while swimming, and keep the duration of the swim short. It is important to not exhaust dogs that are swimming, because of the danger of drowning.

Walking is excellent exercise for the senior dog, as well as for her owner. Although walking places a greater impact on dogs' joints than does swimming, walking can also strengthen leg muscles as well as provide a good endurance workout. Walk at a pace that is comfortable for the senior dog, and limit the walk's duration to what she is capable of without overexertion.

Walk at a comfortable pace for the senior dog.

100. Sports for Seniors

Some sports activities have special competitive classes for senior dogs to participate in. For example, in agility, dogs over a certain age may compete at a lower jump height and they may be allowed more time to complete the course to obtain a qualifying score. Two sports activities that dogs can begin and compete in successfully during their senior years are rally obedience and tracking.

Rally obedience is an excellent sport for senior dogs. It allows them to use their mind and training to compete and interact with their owner. In AKC rally competition, the novice level does not require jumping, so the senior dog can negotiate this level easily.

Tracking is another great sport to begin with an older dog. They take the lead, and do not follow verbal commands from the handler, so even if they are beginning to lose their hearing, they can still track.

Conclusion

Keeping dogs physically active and engaged is fun and beneficial for both dogs and owners. Training exercises, behaviors, and skills needed for sports and other activities will keep dogs and owners fit and alert throughout their lives.

Exercise and activity are two important pieces of your lifestyle. Part III discusses another vital piece: diet and nutrition. A dog's fitness level depends a great deal on his weight. Underweight dogs have problems with strength and stamina. Overweight dogs face problems ranging from overstressed joints and organs to a susceptibility to severe illnesses, such as diabetes and heart disease. How much to feed is as important as the kind of food dogs are fed. Part III presents a few considerations for choosing the feeding method that works for both you and your dog.

The last section in Part III covers injury prevention and illnesses that pertain specifically to exercising and physical activity in dogs. Signs to look for and what to do about bone, muscle, and joint injuries are presented, as well as illness brought on by sustained physical activity—hyperthermia, hypothermia, and dehydration. Immediate response and treatment must always be followed by a trip to your veterinarian or animal hospital as soon as possible.

PART III

your dog's
FITNESS
lifestyle

Considering a Lifestyle Change

Side view of a lean and fit dog

Top view of a lean and fit dog

Before beginning any sports activity or drastic change in daily activity, the dog's general health and weight must be evaluated. Active dogs need to be trim and lean with defined muscle and very little fat. Overweight dogs can be more easily injured during strenuous activities, due to extra weight on their bones and joints and additional stress on their cardiovascular system. If the dog is determined to be overweight, his calorie intake must be lowered and any sports or activity program must be adjusted to his fitness level.

Competition and performance activities require more strength and endurance than is required of the average house dog. An honest evaluation of the dog's weight is very important. Run one hand across the dog's back from the shoulder blades to the pelvic bones and up high on the rib cage. Dogs tend to gain weight on their back first. If the dog is overweight, you will be able to feel the fat on his back, along the spine, over the pelvic bones and hips, and on the rib cage from the spine downward. In a dog of healthy weight, you should be able to feel the dog's shoulder blades, spine, and pelvic bones without having to press down with any firmness. The bones should be prominent without jutting. You should also be able to feel the dog's rib cage, just below the spine, without pressure.

The performance dog is an athlete and needs to be in the same physical shape as humans need to be for running marathons, sprinting, tennis, football, swimming, or any other sports activity. Consider how trim and fit Olympic and professional athletes are—that is what the canine athlete should strive for.

Evaluating Diet and Nutrition

A balanced, highly nutritious diet is the foundation upon which to build a healthy lifestyle for your dog. Diet plays a key role in keeping dogs fit and trim. A lean, fit dog is able to play games and sports for longer periods of time without fatigue or injury, and can recover from the effects of strenuous activity back to normal quickly—a good indicator of a healthy cardiovascular system.

There are four basic methods for feeding dogs: (1) commercially processed kibble or canned food, (2) a homemade cooked or raw diet, (3) commercially made raw food, or (4) a combination of the three. Whether the food is processed or homemade, the most important considerations are whether it offers balanced nutrition and suits your individual dog. Choosing what works best for each dog is a decision the dog's owner needs to make in conjunction with the dog's veterinarian.

Some dogs have food allergies and/or digestion-related illnesses. Specific food allergies are not uncommon among dogs. Excessive scratching that results in skin lesions is a good indication that the dog is having an allergic reaction to something in her diet. Trying foods with different ingredients may help decipher the problem. Also, a simple blood test available through your veterinarian can identify possible sources of allergies. If the test shows an allergy to certain foods, an easy remedy would be to eliminate those items from her diet.

Balanced nutrition is important for healthy, growing puppies.

Dry Dog Food, or Kibble

Commercially processed kibble is used by the majority of pet owners for their dog's nutrition. Convenience, cost, and the wide variety of kibble available are cited in choosing this diet. There are many types of kibble: premium, high-quality kibble for performance dogs; brand-name kibble usually found in pet and grocery stores; and store-brand, generic kibble. There are different recipes for dogs with allergies and different nutritional formulas for puppies, adults, and senior dogs. There are different formulas for large dogs and small dogs, and even breed-specific kibble. Today, you can also find kibble that is grain free, kibble made for high-energy dogs, kibble made from organic ingredients, and even kibble that includes holistic remedies. Choosing the diet that is right for the canine athlete is particular to each individual dog and his needs. The dog's owner and veterinarian are the best people to evaluate the dog's nutritional needs.

GUIDELINES IN CHOOSING KIBBLE

- Select the highest-quality food you can afford. Look for quality ingredients with animal sources of protein and fat high on the list of ingredients (the first two or three items). Expect to pay for quality. Poor-quality foods, which contain a high percentage of grains such as corn, which keep the dog feeling full, do not digest completely and lead to fewer important nutrients being absorbed. Ultimately, paying for higher-quality food is more cost-effective.

- Avoid brightly colored dry foods. These may look attractive to the owner, but the fact is that dogs do not see color and will be consuming unhealthy, unnecessary chemicals used to dye the kibble.

- Look for the expiration date on the label. Most dry dog food has a shelf life of one year, in ideal conditions (cool, dry storage). If it smells bad, looks off-color, or feels too greasy or crumbly, it has probably oxidized into something unpalatable for your dog.

- Check the label for a combination of natural antioxidants: vitamin E (tocopherols), vitamin C (ascorbic acid), rosemary extract, and citric acid. Antioxidants block the oxidation of fats, preventing the formation of peroxides and hydroperoxides, which can be harmful to dogs' health.

- Avoid holistic brands that contain garlic or avocado, which are toxic to dogs.

Use the information on the label to determine the proper amount of food to feed. These are only guidelines because each dog has individual nutritional needs. A 50-pound (22.7 kilogram) house dog may only require 1,400 calories per day to maintain body weight, whereas a working dog may require up to 2,100 calories per day. Adjust the amount of food to the activity level of the dog.

If the dog is overweight, decrease the amount of food given by at least one-quarter on a weekly basis, until you see the dog losing weight. Once the dog reaches the desired weight, increase the amount of food slightly to hold that weight. Feeling and weighing the dog every other day can help determine whether he is gaining or losing weight.

Canned Dog Food

Although canned dog food may seem more appealing for dogs, it does not offer very many advantages over dry dog food. Most canned food contains up to 75 percent water, so the dog is getting less meat/nutrients than he would from kibble. Canned foods are usually more expensive to feed than dry dog food, especially for larger breeds. However, the texture of canned food is very appealing to most dogs. Canned food is usually recommended for dogs recovering from illness or surgery because of its high palatability.

GUIDELINES IN CHOOSING CANNED FOOD

- Be sure to choose one that is labeled prominently with its primary ingredient, for example, "beef" or "chicken" or "lamb"—if such words are used only as modifiers, there is less meat in the can. For example, if the can is labeled "beef dinner" or "beef entrée," the food must only contain 25 percent meat by weight. But if it is labeled simply "beef," the can must contain 70 percent beef by weight. Read the label carefully to ensure your dog gets the proper nutrition.

- Look for cans labeled "nutritionally complete and balanced" for food with all the vitamins, minerals, and nutrients recommended for dogs. Food labeled "canned meat products" is not formulated to be nutritionally complete and is intended to supplement/increase the amount of protein or fat in the dog's meal.

- Canned dog food has a shelf life of about two years. The listed ingredients are blended together and heated, canned, and then pressure cooked for up to one hour. Check to see that the can is not damaged, to ensure the integrity of the product inside.

Homemade Diets: Cooked and Raw Food

Feeding a homemade diet is more costly and time-consuming than feeding a commercial kibble diet. In addition to time spent actually buying and preparing the meals, pet owners considering this option must spend time educating themselves on the nutritional value of the foods they feed, in addition to the nutritional requirements of their dog. Finding a recipe that ensures the dog a nutritionally balanced diet can be difficult. Refer to page 166 for books and websites with recipes. Be sure to avoid recipes that contain substances toxic to dogs, such as garlic, onions, or chocolate. Dogs with allergies can benefit from home-made diets because the owner has complete control over the

Raw diets often include raw bones.

ingredients and can avoid those ingredients causing the allergic reaction.

Homemade (cooked and raw food) diets require vitamin and mineral supplements to make them nutritionally balanced. An added cost may include dietary analysis to ensure proper nutrition. All commercial dog foods that claim to be completely balanced must contain ten amino acids, one essential fatty acid, twelve minerals, and twelve vitamins. These nutrients are needed in the homemade diet as well.

CONSIDERATIONS IN CHOOSING A HOMEMADE DIET

- Are there readily available, trustworthy sources to purchase fresh meats and vegetables at reasonable cost and sufficient quantities to make up daily meals?

- Do you have a recipe for a mixture that provides a nutritionally balanced meal with appropriate vitamin and mineral supplements?

- Are you willing and able to follow specific handling and storage instructions to minimize bacterial contamination of raw foods? You will need to keep any meats frozen until ready to use, thaw them in the refrigerator, clean all preparation surfaces and feeding bowls thoroughly, and refrigerate or discard leftovers promptly.

Commercial Raw Food Diet

Raw food diets are controversial, but they have been rising in popularity. Some veterinarians and holistic veterinarians recommend the raw diet. Other more traditional veterinarians do not encourage it. The raw diet gives the owner complete control over the type of ingredients, their freshness, and their quality. They can eliminate preservatives and chemicals in the dog's food and control more precisely vitamin and other supplements. Most raw diet advocates believe that dogs are able to digest raw food much easier than cooked or processed food and are therefore better able to process the nutrients in the food more completely.

A variety of commercial raw diets are sold at many pet stores. The meat mixtures are frozen; they can be thawed and fed as is. Some products are supplemented with a regulated combination of vitamins and minerals. They provide a complete nutritional food source. Others require vitamin and mineral supplements to formulate a nutritionally balanced diet. Raw diets provide the same types of food for all of the dog's life stages. Changes are made in the amount of food and supplements to accommodate the needs of puppies, adults and seniors.

Combination Diets

A combination of commercial dry food (kibble) and fresh ingredients is a viable alternative for many pet owners. Fresh ingredients such as cottage cheese, ricotta cheese, plain yogurt, spinach, green beans, and other vegetables (pulverized or mashed) can be added to kibble for extra nutrition. (Dogs don't have the enzyme required to break open cell walls and release nutrients in most plant foods, so a food processor or juicer should be used.) These fresh foods must not be mistaken for "people foods," such as hamburger sandwich, muffins, fried bacon or chicken, spaghetti, and other leftover foods from the owners' meals. Spices, seasonings, ingredients in the onion family, cooking methods, and added fats and sugars used in food preparation for people (primarily to enhance taste) can lead to digestive problems and illness in dogs. This practice also adds empty calories to the dog's diet and contributes to weight problems.

How Often to Feed

It takes approximately twenty-two hours for dogs to completely digest their food. Many people feed their dogs once daily, either in the morning or evening, whichever fits their household schedule. Twice a day, morning and evening, is often followed by people who give supplements or medication to their dog (usually recommended to be taken with food). Or, they like to have their dogs eat when they do. Remember to feed the correct amount of food, however many times the dog is fed (for example, feed half the amount of food if given twice a day). Also include the amount of treats the dog is given in the daily calorie count. Some dog trainers use the dog's meal kibble as treats, setting aside some of the meal to use for training during the day.

It is not a good idea to free feed a dog. Free feeding (always having food available) leads to weight gain and training problems. Food loses its value as a reward if the dog is never hungry enough to work for it. The dog's digestive system is also taxed, because it is always working to digest food.

Water, Water, Water

Fresh, clean water should be available at all times, both inside the house and outdoors. It should be refilled daily, and the bowls cleaned regularly to prevent bacteria and mold from growing and being ingested. Good hydration is very important to maintaining healthy muscles and during recovery from illness or injury.

Always provide an abundance of clean, fresh water.

Preventing Injuries

There is always a risk of injury or illness during rigorous physical activities. It is important that dog owners be aware of what can happen and uses precautions to ensure their pet's safety. Common sense and care must be taken to avoid potential problems and stay safe.

First and foremost, the dog should be seen by a veterinarian for a health and wellness exam before beginning any exercise or fitness program. The vet should be told which type of activities the dog will be involved in and how often. The vet will be able to ascertain whether the dog is physically able to perform the activities.

To recognize a problem and respond quickly to possible injury or illness, pet owners must be familiar with how their pet looks and acts *normally*. Observe how the dog breathes, eats, drinks, walks, sleeps, urinates, and defecates, and note her usual energy level and interest in engaging with you. Keen observation of the dog's normal habits and movements will make the owner more sensitive to any changes that may signal illness or injury.

Be informed about the types of injuries associated with the sport or activity chosen for the dog. Once these sources are identified, the owner can be attentive to the dog for any signs of injury or illness (fatigue or lameness). Knowledge of possible safety issues will also help in assembling a first-aid kit to have on hand so if an injury does occur, the owner is prepared to help the dog.

Strains, Sprains, and Tendinitis

A *strain* is an injury to a muscle. A *sprain* is an injury to a ligament or joint capsule. Ligaments are tissues that connect bone to bone or bone to muscle. Tendons are bands of fibrous connective tissue that connect muscle to bone. *Tendonitis* is the stretching, tearing, or partial rupturing of a tendon.

Strains can be caused by prolonged stress or overexertion of the muscle, trauma to the muscle, or sudden stretching of the muscle fibers. Common symptoms include lameness, swelling or knotting of the muscle, and tenderness over the injured area. Rest and cold packs are recommended to treat a muscle strain. Cold packs should be applied for 5 to 15 minutes, three to five times per day. Acupuncture treatments can also be helpful to promote the healing of a torn or strained muscle.

Sprains are an injury to the joint capsule or the ligaments caused by sudden stretching or tearing of the joint capsule or ligament. The symptoms of a sprain include pain over the joint, swelling of the tissues, limitation of motion, and lameness. The most important treatment for a sprain is rest. If the ligament is torn, the joint should be immobilized by splinting. Cold packs are applied to the joint to manage swelling. Apply the cold pack for 5 to 20 minutes every hour for the first 3 hours. Thereafter apply cold packs three to five times per day. Acupuncture treatments can help promote healing. All activity related to the joint should be stopped and the joint should be rested. In some cases, if the ligament is completely torn, surgery can be an option. Torn ligaments of the knee can be repaired by orthopedic surgery.

Quick Injury Diagnostic Guide

INJURY	DEFINITION	SYMPTOMS	TREATMENT
Strain	Injury to a muscle	Lameness, swelling or knotting of muscle, and tenderness	Rest and cold packs
Sprain	Injury to a ligament or joint capsule	Pain over the joint, swelling of tissues, limitation of motion, and lameness	Rest injured joint. Cold packs to manage swelling.
Tendonitis	Stretching, tearing, or partial rupturing of a tendon	Lameness, pain on standing, swelling over the tendon	Rest and limited use of affected joint

Tendonitis is caused by sudden twisting of the limb or overuse of the limb from strenuous activities. Lameness, pain on standing (weight bearing), and swelling over the tendon area are signs of tendonitis. Rest and very limited use of the affected joint is required to heal tendonitis. A complete rupture of a tendon must be repaired surgically.

Medication for strains, sprains, and tendonitis should be avoided or used cautiously. Medication that relieves discomfort will encourage the dog to use the limb and will not allow him to rest the injury. Limping caused by these injuries is an important indicator of the healing process, because the dog limps to protect the limb from further injury. This helps determine whether the injury is healing.

Treating Illness

In addition to the above-mentioned injuries, dogs as well as their owners can succumb to illness brought on by environmental factors during their outside activities. The most common illnesses affecting canine athletes are hyperthermia (overheating), hypothermia (becoming too cold), and dehydration. Although the following discussion includes immediate treatments for these life-threatening conditions, stricken dogs should be taken to a veterinarian for a complete exam as soon as possible.

Signs of Heatstroke

- Bright red gum color in early stages; pale, blue, or gray in late stages
- Panting heavily; thick saliva
- Body temperature above 104°F (40°C)
- Increased heart rate and respiratory rate
- Disorientation, "drunken" behavior, depression
- Vomiting or diarrhea, with or without the presence of blood
- Capillary refill time is too fast
- Shock
- Collapse, coma

Immediate first aid and veterinary treatment are essential.

Hyperthermia

Heatstroke, or hyperthermia, can occur when dogs are exercised excessively in hot weather, or any time they are not acclimated to warm weather. Heavily coated or short-muzzled dogs (such as bulldogs) are more susceptible to overheating. Dogs that have had heat stroke previously are also at a higher risk for hyperthermia.

Rapid breathing or panting is used by dogs to exchange hot air for cool air, to regulate their body temperature. When the air temperature equals a dog's body temperature, cooling by rapid breathing does not work and she begins to overheat.

Signs of Shock

Early Shock
- Increased heart rate and pulse
- Reddish gum color
- Capillary refill time of 1 to 2 seconds
- "Pounding" pulse

Middle Stages
- Low body temperature
- Cool limbs and pads
- Weak, rapid pulse
- Pale gums/mucous membranes
- Slow capillary refill time (more than 3 seconds)
- Woozy, weakened mental state

Late Stages
- Slow respiratory and heart rate
- Weak or no pulse
- Depressed mental state, unconsciousness
- Stopped breathing, cardiac arrest

Immediate first aid and veterinary treatment are essential.

Symptoms of hyperthermia include excessive rapid, frantic, noisy panting; bright red tongue and gums; thick saliva; increased heart rate; stupor (stumbling with a vacant expression); vomiting; and diarrhea. A dog experiencing hyperthermia will have a rectal temperature of 106°F (41.1°C) or higher.

If a dog is experiencing hyperthermia, emergency measures must begin at once. It is critical to reduce the dog's body temperature to 104°F (40°C) within 10 to 15 minutes, to avoid coma and possibly death.

Mild cases of overheating will respond to being moved into an air-conditioned area. More extreme cases may require immersion in a cold water bath or hosing down with cold water. Wet towels placed on the dog's head, neck, chest, feet, and abdomen can cool her body down quickly. Use a fan to blow cool air on the dog's face to help her breath in cooler air to lower her body temperature. A cold water enema will lower her body temperature very rapidly.

Continue to monitor the dog's temperature. When it lowers to 104°F (40°C), the cooling process should be stopped. Take the dog to a veterinary hospital immediately, because the conditions caused by hyperthermia can recur.

Consequences of hyperthermia include kidney failure, problems with blood clotting, neurological problems (including swelling of the brain and seizures), abnormal heart rhythm, respiratory arrest, and destruction of the lining of the digestive tract.

Hypothermia

Dogs suffering from hypothermia can be shivering, staggering, or lethargic. In extreme cases, the dog could be unconscious or having seizures. Move the dog immediately to a warm location and dry him if he is wet. Wrap the dog in warm towels or blankets and offer warm water or warm chicken broth to encourage drinking. Wrap a warm water bottle in a towel and place it next to the dog's belly, or if there is a heating pad available, turn it to its lowest setting and place it over him. Keep warming and checking on the dog until his temperature reaches 100°F (38°C). Have the dog checked by a veterinarian as soon as possible.

Dehydration

Dehydration is caused by an excessive loss of body fluids. Dogs can experience dehydration if they are involved in active physical exercise throughout the day and are not drinking enough water. Symptoms include listlessness and stupor, loss of skin elasticity, dry mouth,

and in its later stages, circulatory collapse. Preventing dehydration is simple—have clean drinking water available at all times and monitor the amount of water the dog is drinking, especially on warm days.

Treatment for dehydration is directed at preventing further loss of body fluids and replacing fluids. In mild cases, giving an electrolyte solution, such as Pedialyte, can hydrate the dog. In more extreme cases, subcutaneous fluids are used to hydrate the dog. If a dog is dehydrated, seek veterinary attention as soon as possible.

Extreme cold temperatures can cause dogs to suffer from hypothermia. Even dogs with heavy coats can be affected.

Resources and References

AGILITY

The following is a list of organizations which sponsor agility trials. Each organization has a list of local clubs and events on their website, as well as rules and regulations governing agility trials held under their sponsorship.

American Kennel Club (AKC)
www.akc.org

Australian Shepherd Club of America (ASCA)
www.asca.org

Canine Performance Events (CPE)
www.k9cpe.com

North American Dog Agility Council (NADAC)
www.nadac.com

United States Dog Agility Association (USDAA)
www.usdaa.com

FINDING AGILITY TRAINING CLASSES

Clean Run, "The Magazine for Dog Agility Enthusiasts," has been in publication since 1995 and is the resource for news and information about agility for the agility competitor. It provides online services which include a listing for agility training classes throughout the United States.

- See their website at www.cleanrun.com
  Select: Events, clubs & training links, state, services (any, agility classes, private lessons, facility rental, indoor/outdoor training, wheel-chair access, or other), affiliation, (select any)

The American Kennel Club (AKC) offers a listing of AKC clubs which offer agility training.

- See their website at www.akc.org
  Select: Answer center, other common questions, miscellaneous, dog training, How do I find an AKC Club that offers dog training? Select: AKC clubs that offer training classes: Click on state for listing by city within selected state.

FINDING A LOCAL AGILITY CLUB

Clean Run also provides a listing of agility organizations in the United States, Canada, and overseas. Each organization offers listings of clubs by state, region, or postal code.

- See their website at www.cleanrun.com
  Select: Events, agility organizations (Listing of agility organizations in the United States, Canada, and overseas.

- See their website at www.akc.org
  Select: Club search, agility clubs, select state for alphabetical listing by name of clubs within the state.

- See their website at www.asca.org
  Select: ASCA Information, affiliate clubs for listing by state.

- See their website at www.nadac.com
  Select: Clubs, find a NADAC Club (choose listing in alphabetical order by club name or listing by postal code)

- See their website at www.usda.com
  Select: General information, group locator, select a region for the alphabetical listing of clubs by state within the selected region.

FINDING AN AGILITY EVENT

Attending an agility trial is a good way to get local information and experience the excitement of agility competition. Trials showcase the bond between the handler and the dog, the teamwork involved in navigating the course successfully, and the enjoyment by both of the sport.

- See their website at www.akc.org
  Select: Event and awards search, time range, agility rrials, and state (produces listing of trials by date).

- See their website at www.asca.org
  Select: Events, show trials newsletter, select (latest date), trials listed by type of event (agility, conformation, obedience, tracking, stock, ranch), date and state.

- See their website at www.k9cpe.com
  Select: Events, listing by date, state, and city.

- See their website at www.nadac.com
  Select: Calendars, listing of NADAC trials, (Fill in state and date range).

- See their website at www.usda.com
  Select: News & events, events calendar, list of all events (or by titling categories).

- Cited reference: "Everything you always wanted to know about agility: What are the most common breeds competing in agility?" by Brenna Fender, *Clean Run*, Vol 15, No. 8 August 2009 issue, page 7.

HERDING

There are many organizations which sponsor herding trials, including:

American Kennel Club (AKC)
www.akc.org

Australian Shepherd Club of America (ASCA)
www.asca.org

American Herding Breed Association
www.ahba-herding.org

United States Border Collie Handlers Association
www.usbcha.com

OBEDIENCE

The following is a list of organizations which sponsor obedience trials:

American Kennel Club (AKC)
www.akc.org

Australian Shepherd Club of America (ASCA)
www.asca.org

United Kennel Club (UKC)
www.ukcdogs.com

Australian National Kennel Council (ANKC)
www.ankc.org.au

Canadian Kennel Club (CKC)
www.ckc.ca

CANINE FREESTYLE

There are several organizations regulating competitive freestyle. They include:

World Canine Freestyle Organization (WCFO)
www.worldcaninefreestyle.org

Canine Freestyle Federation (CFF)
www.canine-freestyle.org

The Musical Dog Sport Association (MDSA)
www.musicaldogsport.org

Paws 2 Dance Canine Freestyle Organization Canada
www.paws2dance.com

Canine Freestyle GB
Great Britain
www.caninefreestylegb.com

Pawfect K9 Freestyle Club
Japan
www.pawfect.jp

RALLY OBEDIENCE

The following is a list of organizations which sponsor rally trials:

American Kennel Club (AKC)
www.akc.org

Canadian Kennel Club (CKC)
www.ckc.ca

DISC DOG

Ashley Whippet Invitational—The *Canine Frisbee Disc World Championship,* also called the World Finals Championship, was long considered the crowning culmination of the sport.

- See their website at www.ashleywhippet.com

Skyhoundz—This organization runs its own championship event, known as the *Hyperflite Skyhoundz World Canine Disc Championships.*

- See their website at www.skyhoundz.com

UFO—UFO sponsors a points series called the *UFO World Cup Series,* which culminates in a World Cup final.

- See their website at www.ufoworldcup.org

U.S. Disc Dog Nationals—USDDN clubs organize events in the United Sates, Japan, the Netherlands, Germany, Poland, Canada, and Australia. It sponsors a championship series known as the *USDDN Finals* and *US Disc Dog International Finals.*

- See their website at www.usddn.com

Other disc dog competitions are sponsored by the Quadruped, the International Disc Dog Handlers' Association (IDDHA), the Flying Disc Dog Open, and the Purina Incredible Dog Challenge.

FLYBALL

- See their website at www.flyball.com

SCENT HURDLES

Canadian Kennel Club (CKC)
www.ckc.ca

TRACKING

Johhson, Glen R., *Tracking Dog, Theory and Methods,* Fifth Edition, 2003 Revised, Barkleigh Productions, Inc., Mechanicsburgh, PA, 1975 (first printing).

Sanders, William R. (Sil), *Enthusiastic Tracking, The Step-by-Step Training Handbook,* Second Edition, Rime Publications, Stanwood, WA 1998.

There are a few organizations which have tracking titling programs, including:

American Kennel Club (AKC)

www.akc.org

Australian Shepherd Club of America (ASCA)

www.asca.org

United Kennel Club (UKC)

www.ukcdogs.com

DOCK DIVING

These are organizations that promote the sport of dock diving:

Dog Dogs

www.dockdogs.com

Splash Dogs

www.splashdogs.com

Ultimate Air Dogs (UKC titling)

www.ultimateairdogs.net

Super Retriever Series

www.superretrieverseries.com

CARTING

Titling in draft work or carting is awarded through breed clubs:

Bernese Mountain Dog Club

www.bmdca.org

Greater Swiss Mountain Dog Club of America

www.gsmdca.org

Newfoundland Dog Club of America

www.ncanewfs.org

Bouvier Club of America

www.bouvier.org

Saint Bernard Club of America

www.saintbernardclub.org

WEIGHT PULLING

International Weight Pulling Association (IWPA)

www.iwpa.net

United Kennel Club (UKC)

www.ukdogs.com

American Dog Breeders Association (ADBA)

www.adba.cc

LURE COURSING

There are several organizations for competition and titling in lure coursing:

American Sighthound Field Association (ASFA)

www.afsa.org

American Kennel Club (AKC)

www.akc.org

Fédération Cynologique Internationale (FCI)

Lure Coursing Fanatics Club (LCF)

www.lurecoursingfanatics.com

Course a'Lure

www.coursealure.com

EARTHDOG

American Kennel Club (AKC)

www.akc.org

The Jack Russell Terrier Club of America (JRTCA)

www.therealjackrussell.com

The American Working Terrier Association (AWTA)

www.dirt-dog.com

Canadian Kennel Club (CKC)

www.ckc.ca

FIELD TRIALS AND HUNT TESTS

Amateur Field Trial Clubs of America (AFTCA)

www.aftca.org

American Kennel Club (AKC)

www.akc.org

North American Versatile Hunting Dog Association (NAVHDA)

www.navhda.org

United Kennel Club (UKC)

www.ukcdogs.com

SLEDDING

International Sled Dog Racing Association

www.isdra.org

SKIJORING

International Sled Dog Racing Association

www.isdra.org

European Sled Dog Racing Association (ESDRA)

www.esdra.net

The International Federation of Sleddog Sports (IFSS)

www.sleddogsport.com

CANICROSS

Dog Run Dog®

www.dogrundog.com

Run Dawg Run

www.rundawgrun.com

K9 NOSE WORK

National Association of Canine Scent Work (NACSW)

www.nacsw.net

HIKING

Visit Your National Parks website at http://www.nps.gov/parks.html

SURFING

Surfin' Paws sponsors events and offers lessons.

- See their website at www.surfinpaws.com.

Surf City surf dog clinics and activities take place at the Dog Beach in Huntington Beach, California.

Reed, Kevin and A.K. Crump, *The Dog's Guide to Surfing,* TCB-Café Publishing, San Francisco, California, copyright 2005.

GENERAL RESOURCES

Dainty, Suellen, *50 Games to Play with Your Dog,* TFH Publications, Neptune City, NJ, 2007.

Dennis, Helen and Liz Dalby, *Happy Dog,* Quintet Publishing, London, UK 2009.

Mehus-Roe, Kristin, *Canine Sports & Games,* Storey Publishing, North Adams, MA 2009.

Saunders, Debbie Gross, *Stretching the Performance Dog,* Clean Run Productions, South Hadley, MA 2005 (DVD).

Saunders, Debbie Gross, *Strengthening the Performance Dog,* Clean Run Productions, South Hadley, MA 2006 (DVD).

Zink, M. Christine, DVM, *The Agility Advantage,* Clean Run Productions, South Hadley, MA 2008.

Zink, M. Christine, DVM, and Laurie McCauley, DVM, *Building the Canine Athlete,* Canine Sports Productions, Ellicott City, MD 2007 (DVD).

Zink, Christine, DVM, and Julie Daniels, *Jumping from A to Z,* Canine Sports Productions, Lutherville, MD, 1996.

Zink, M. Christine, DVM, *Peak Performance,* Canine Sports Productions, Ellicott City, MD 1997, 2000, 2004.

DIET AND NUTRITION

Brevitz, Betsy, DVM, *The Complete Healthy Dog Handbook,* Workman Publishing, New York, NY 2004, 2009.

Jacobs, Jocelynn, DVM, *Performance Dog Nutrition,* Sno Shire Publications, Sanford, MI, 2005.

Lazarus, Pat, *Keep Your Dog Healthy the Natural Way,* Ballantine Publishing Group, New York, 1999.

Pitcairn, Richard H., DVM, and Susan Hubble Pitcairn, *Dr Pitcairn's Complete Guide to Natural Health for Dogs and Cats,* Rodale Press, Inc., Emmaus, PA 1995.

Segal, Monica AHCW, *K9 Kitchen,* Doggie Diner, Inc, Toronto, Canada 2009.

Segal, Monica AHCW, *Optimal Nutrition,* Doggie Diner, Inc, Toronto, Canada 2007.

Volhard, Wendy and Kerry Brown, DVM, *Holistic Guide for a Healthy Dog,* Second Edition, Howell Book House, Foster City, CA 2000.

Yarnall, Celeste, Ph.D., *Natural Dog Care,* Journey Editions, North Clarendon, VT 2000.

The website www.monicasegal.com gives information on dietary supplements for dogs.

The website www.celestialpets.com gives raw food recopies for dogs and cats, as well as information on supplements.

PREVENTING INJURIES AND TREATING ILLNESS

Carlson, Delbert G., DVM, and James M. Giffin, MD, *Dog Owner's Home Veterinary Handbook,* Howell Book House, New York, NY 1992.

Kay, Nancy, *Speaking for Spot,* Trafalgar Square Books, North Pomfret, VT, 2008.

Mammato, Bobbie, DVM, MPH, *Pet First Aid,* Stay Well, Boston MA, copyright 1997 by the American Red Cross and the Humane Society of the United States.

Photographer Credits

All photos by Pam Marks/www.pawprincestudios.com, with the exception of the following:

© ARCO/H. Reinhard/agefotostock.com, 158

© Jean Louis Aubert/agefotostock.com, 88

© Mark J. Barrett/Alamy, 148

Kirsten Cole-MacMurray, 4

Bill Curtsinger/gettyimages.com, 107

© F1online digitale Bildagentur GmbH/Alamy, 10

James Forte/gettyimages.com, 128

LM Gray, 90

© Matt Hage/agefotostock.com, 152

© i love images/Alamy, 8

© imagebroker/Alamy, 161

© Image Source/Alamy, 12

© image100/agefotostock.com, 17

iStockphoto.com, 2; 16; 28 (top); 44; 47; 75; 76; 104; 106; 115; 116; 117; 119; 122; 123; 137; 138; 144; 160; 165

© Juniors Bildarchiv/agefotostock.com, 156

© Juniors Bildarchiv/Alamy, 11

© Kim Karpeles/agefotostock.com, 155

Elyse Lewin/gettyimages.com, 125

Carl Lyttle/gettyimages.com, 120

onEdition Photography/W-W-I.com, 80

Nick Ridley, 102; 103

Pete Saloutos/gettyimages.com, 14

© Stockbyte/agefotostock.com, 124

© Alexander Trocha/agefotostock.com, 66

Kathe Vasquez, 94

© imagebroker/Alamy, 161

John Wagner/Fairbanks Daily News/ZUMA Press, 96

Index

Acknowledgments

Nothing significant is accomplished without the support of family and friends. Sincere thanks to our family, Robert MacMurray, Steve Mitchell, and Samantha Mitchell for their help as models, readers, and critics. Special thanks also to Meredith Catanzaro for stepping in to do chores when deadlines meant long days away from the ranch.

Many thanks to Pam Marks, our fantastic photographer who managed a photo shoot just one week after major surgery.

Thanks to the following friends for supplying our four-legged models (or photos): Marilyn Bennett, Pat Brown, Stacey Fleischer, Daneen Fox, Nancy Gast, Susan Hartzler, Teri Lowe, Lisa Marzban, Julie Sandoval, Lyn Silberer, Kate Smith, and Teresa Vanvranken. Kathe Vasquez (carting); Anne Hershey and Linda Gray (tracking); and Desiree Snelleman (teaching the wave, nosework, and canicross).

Thanks to Sue McMahan for her photo research, and to Marc Marseille and Janelle Fuchigami for sharing their expertise in dock diving. Dr. Susan Meisinger, DC, LAc, QME, reviewed all our stretching exercises. Special thanks to Curt Uritz for introducing us to Dr. Ian Holsworth.

We were also very fortunate in having a thoroughly supportive, patient, and talented team at Quarry Books: Rochelle Bourgault, acquisitions editor; Betsy Gammons, project manager and David Martinell, art director. Their guidance and understanding of conflicting schedules and impending deadlines was invaluable in getting the book done.

About the Authors

Kirsten Cole-MacMurray

Born and raised in Southern California, Kirsten Cole-MacMurray has worked with animals of all stripes, from family pets to large livestock and horses. She has degrees in animal science and Anthropology, specializing in primatology.

In 1980, Kirsten became a professional animal trainer, teaching obedience lessons and in-home problem solving with pets. She raised livestock for competition at county fairs and competed with her horse in endurance races.

Kirsten and her dogs have been actively competing in agility, herding, obedience, and conformation shows since 1994. They have earned top agility honors from the American Kennel Club (AKC), Australian Shepherd Club of America (ASCA), North American Dog Agility Council (NADAC), and United States Dog Agility Association (USDAA).

Kirsten has trained and competed with a variety of dog breeds, including Cocker Spaniel, Doberman Pincher, Miniature Poodle, Border Terrier, Bichon Frise, Border Collie, Golden Retriever, Flat Coat Retriever, Chesapeake Bay Retriever, and a Whippet.

Stephanie Nishimoto

Stephanie Nishimoto grew up on the Big Island of Hawaii, where the family Cocker Spaniel was allowed to roam freely from house to house and only came home for dinner. An interest in dog behavior which began with an Australian Shepherd 12 years ago, has led her into researching dogs' behaviors, health, and fitness. She has been training dogs in agility and obedience in Southern California, since 1998. Stephanie has competed at the ASCA National Australian Shepherd Specialty and completed ASCA Agility Championships with her dogs. She is an AKC Agility Trial Secretary and has organized and acted as the Trial Secretary for ASCA Obedience Trials.